To Laurie 2010
Easter
Love,
Mom and Dad

MANY LANDS
MANY HEARTS

MANY LANDS
MANY HEARTS
MORE THAN A MEMOIR

CHARLES L. FIELDS

Outskirts Press, Inc.
Denver, Colorado

Many Lands Many Hearts
More Than A Memoir

Outskirts Press, Inc.
http://www.outskirtspress.com

ISBN PB: 978-1-4327-5366-5
ISBN HB: 978-1-4327-5385-6

Outskirts Press and the "OP" logo are trademarks belonging to Outskirts Press, Inc.

PRINTED IN THE UNITED STATES OF AMERICA

Table of Contents

Preface

This book is more than a memoir. It is also a collage of travel journals, reflections and observations. Years ago I joined a group of aspiring writers who exchanged e-mails describing various experiences. Fashioning ourselves after the famous writers who frequented New York's Algonquin Hotel, we formed the Literary Knights of the Round Table. Feeding one another's egos, we thought that someday we might assemble these exchanges into a book. Unfortunately, because of deaths and other types of partings, the group broke up. I continued a daily writing regimen and finally, with the courage to stand alone, make this presentation to an unknown field of readers. As for my travels across America, others such as John Steinbeck, William Least-Heat-Moon and Jack Kerouac have been there with *Travels with Charlie, Blue Highways,* and *On the Road,* but everyone has his own song to sing and here is mine.

Since retiring from the lobster and chicken business, I have lived on the coast of Massachusetts in the summer and wintered in Arizona. This lifestyle has provided many cross country experiences. With a keen eye for the land and its people, I have tried to capture the pulse and spectrum in a manner that would be informative, amusing, and in some cases reflective. I hope the reader will come on board and enjoy the ride.

Along with the cross-country trips there are interesting side adventures and commentary on timely events to paint a full mural. Our dog, Daisy, accompanied my wife and me on many trips and she receives prominent recognition. The journey continues, but it is time to gather the words and pages and weave the past and present into *Many Lands Many Hearts*.

I pay tribute to my fellow Knights, who gave me not only inspiration but also joyful camaraderie. Thanks go to fellow Knights, the late Lawrence Marsden, author of *Gemini Ship*; the late Donald "Ben" Hogan, author of *Letters to Lou*; Paul "Bad-dog" Driscoll, and Wallace "Wally" Bartlett.

Part One:
Early Days

1

The Other Cape

I was born under the sign of Leo in 1936, on the crest of a wave off Cape Ann, Massachusetts. My mother always refuted this claim, but for my sense of destined greatness I needed a dramatic birthplace. My earliest recollections are side-by-side homes at 47 and 49 Granite Street in Rockport. One was a towering three-story frame overlooking Back Beach and the harbor, the other a two-story dwarf in which anyone taller than six feet had to stoop in the upstairs area and scrunch down in the bathroom. We rented the first house before World War II and the second one after the war, moving to Lynn for a two-year period in between. My father, after a long naval career, was too old for reenlistment and went to work for General Electric. The commute was tiring and time consuming, so the move was necessary.

City living was quite different from life in a quaint seaside village, even though our new home was in a residential area. The house was owned by a Greek family. I still recall the music, cooking aromas, bountiful grape arbor, and different languages. It was like being in another country. I think the constant music helped me in later years to easily master intricate Greek dance steps.

As a young boy getting ready to enter grade school, I found further ethnic exposure in the neighborhood. My new friends Frankie, Benny, Chang, Georgie, and Mike came from Irish, Jewish, Chinese, Greek, and Polish backgrounds: the neighborhood was like the League of Nations. Childhood camaraderie also helped me in my life to deal with human relations problems.

I attended a kindergarten in Rockport, but my first public grade schooling was in Lynn. These years usually have difficulties; mine were compounded by a midyear school change. Our school was taken over by the Army for recruitment, and one morning we all had to march along the sidewalk to another school about two miles away. Fear of the unknown was preeminent, but the chafing of my corduroy knickers was even more annoying. As it turned out, the school had nicer facilities than its predecessor and our teacher was nicer, too.

My memories of the early war years include blackouts, ration stamps, and the influence of the music and propaganda movies of the time. Every Saturday we all walked to the Uptown Theater and viewed a newsreel, two cartoons, and a full-length movie for only ten cents. It was a shock when the cost went to eleven cents. We had to collect more deposit bottles to offset the added expense!

Apparently life in the city did not appeal to my parents, for we soon moved back to Rockport. Fortunately the house next door to our former house was for rent. It was much smaller, but I was glad to be in the old neighborhood. The only uncomfortable thing was facing another midyear school change. I can vividly recall the first day. As I entered the school yard, I felt like an alien intruding on a WASP youth gathering. Even though I knew some of the kids from kindergarten, I sensed that I was being tested. The first attack came from the school bully. Despite my smaller size, my acquired city street smarts proved valuable; I defeated and humiliated him sufficiently so that all schoolyard problems ended that day. I made new friends and passed readily through the various grades.

On September 2, 1945, the loud speaker informed us that the war was over. We were released early and everyone ran pell-mell through the streets shouting "Victory, Victory!" The big kids threw rolls of toilet paper into the trees and telephone wires in harmless wild celebration. The town was a festive microcosm of the whole country. The troops returned and major postwar adjustments began for everyone.

The GI Bill provided free education for many veterans, and housing projects were created that made homes affordable. The newly expanded peacetime workforce created added employment pressure. My father went through many interruptive union strikes, and as a family we had to deal with unsettled economic times.

Without the nursing home facilities available today, the responsibility for my grandmother was shared by my aunts. When it became the obligation of my mother, we had to make a major shift in our three small bedrooms. My mother and father shared the big bed in one bedroom and set up my younger brother and me in twin beds in another. That left my room available for my grandmother.

Nana was an interesting old Irish woman who read tea leaves and never let her long dress rise above her ankles unless she heard a lively jig. Her gums ached from rotten teeth and we children were often sent to the beach at low tide to gather a special sea moss.

Through some kind of poultice preparation the moss provided some comfort. The night Nana died, my brother and I witnessed her being carried out of the house through our bedroom. It was our first experience with death. After what my mother called a cold Catholic ceremony, John and I once again had separate rooms.

The downstairs area comprised a kitchen with a stove fueled by a kerosene jug and a dining room that opened to a small living room. We shared many enjoyable evenings here as a family gathered around the Philco radio. A coal-fired furnace was located in the basement, and one of my chores was to sift the ashes to save any reusable coal. My father had a work bench there where he built lobster traps, and I commandeered a small storeroom for my sanctuary.

The cold war with Russia was developing. A local Jim Crow uprising made me aware my little town was not as innocent and insulated from prejudice as I had thought. I entered junior high school and found myself more interested in athletics than in scholarly pursuits. The summers were filled with days at the beach or skinny dipping at the nearby quarries, caddying at the local golf club, and playing baseball - which was becoming a passion with me.

During the freshman year at Rockport High School my father became ill with a kidney disease and was eventually bedridden. Only a few life saving machines were available at the time. Due to my father's illness my mother had to go to work in the Gloucester fish packing plants. John and I were more or less left to fend for ourselves. Fortunately the neighborhood was made up of artists, engineers, radio announcers, retired insurance executives and even the chief of police. Without the knowledge my brother and I were being observed and guided by these fine people.

THE OTHER CAPE

I am particularly grateful to the nationally recognized artist Aldro Hibbard. He had a son my age and we were both very sports minded. Mr. Hibbard was also manager of the local semipro baseball team. Every Sunday I helped carry all the equipment and for fifty cents was responsible for collecting the foul balls or operating the manual scoreboard. Young Hibbard and I also had free run of his large studio and we played many competitive Ping-Pong matches. Once when we were playing darts, a bad throw went into a new oil painting. I pulled out the dart and desperately pushed fresh paint into the hole. Mr. Hibbard was a National Academician and his paintings were highly collectible. I wonder to this day where that beautiful Vermont mountain snow scene is hanging. Hibbard also gave me great encouragement regarding my baseball talent. I made the high school varsity team and played second base for the American Legion in the Cape Ann Summer League. Unfortunately my father died before my sophomore year. My coach, Raymond "Tink" Hale, stepped in and became a comforting mentor.

In my little basement sanctuary I studied navigation and the names of all the various sails. I dreamed of attending the U.S. Naval Academy, perhaps to carry on my father's love of the navy. He was always upset that he had only served in peacetime between the two world wars and was unable to reenlist. My other dream was to carry my baseball to a more competitive level. At the time, Gloucester High School had a junior ROTC program, better college preparatory classes than Rockport's, and a fine sports program. I started to take control of my destiny. A month into my sophomore year, I asked my mother's permission to transfer to Gloucester High. There was a modest out-of-town tuition fee, but a small settlement from my father's life insurance made it possible to attend.

Entering this city school with what appeared to be an enormous enrollment was difficult, but I soon made many new friends. I joined the baseball team and found that my previous dedicated practice helped me to qualify for the varsity. With new confidence I also joined the football team. "Tink" Hale, my American Legion coach, got me a summer job at the Rockport Golf Club as caddy master and assistant manager of the pro shop. I spent seven days a week at the country club and every evening either playing or practicing baseball.

Junior year started with a full schedule of college prep classes, football practice, and hitchhiking five miles home to Rockport each night. I weighed less than 150 pounds and was not a starter, but always gave 100-percent effort. After another summer of baseball and work at the golf club, I entered my senior year.

I think all schools are filled with cliques. GHS was no exception with the popular jocks, the vocational shop boys, and Italian or Portuguese groups. My diverse childhood exposure in Lynn paid off; I found myself comfortable with all of them and was elected class president. It was hard to believe that this happened to a relative newcomer from Rockport.

All was going well, but with just average grades and no political sponsor, plans for the Naval Academy were ruled out. As a student athlete, I worked to achieve acceptance and a scholarship to a good college. The football season proved to be exciting and rewarding, for I was now the starting right halfback on a single-wing team. My scoring was limited because the left halfback was a superstar who deservedly got all the glory. He later went on to play college ball and had a tryout once with the Detroit Lions. My best girlfriend had recently graduated and was enrolled in a Boston nursing school. We saw each other on weekends, but in that I did not have a car, transportation was difficult. I awkwardly accompanied her parents when they drove her back to Boston.

As senior year came to a close, our baseball team won a division championship. Through my American Legion coach and some of his country club friends, I received a full scholarship to the University of New Hampshire. I had bigger dreams, but the reality was that I had no money.

Graduation went well. My mother, brother and girlfriend attended. The next day I went back to summer work at the golf club. I played ball for the Legion team and for the town team on Sundays. It was great to be playing at last with semipros. I was made aware of the Francis Ouimet Caddy Scholarships, and the club was willing to sponsor me as a candidate. Francis Ouimet came from a caddy background and as a 20-year-old amateur won the 1913 U.S. Open. He beat the two best professional players of the time, Harry Vardon and Ted Ray.

I was awarded one of the scholarships and it turned out that all my expenses to any school in the country were covered. It was almost August and most schools had filled their quotas, but the Ouimet board being Ivy League inclined, it arranged an interview for me at Harvard. Although the session went well, they called to the director of admissions at Brown University and arranged an interview there for later that day. I took the next train to Providence and had a successful meeting, but I had reservations about the school. Something did not appeal to me. I took the application home and started researching other schools.

I thought it best to get out of the New England area and selected Duke University. It was considered the Harvard of the South. In addition, I was interested in parapsychology and Dr. J.B. Rhine was one of the leaders in this field. Duke had established a great baseball program under the legendary Jack Coombs. My Legion coach had attended the University of Alabama and played under Wallace Wade, who later went to Duke as athletic director. The current football and baseball stadiums bear their names. With these connections, letters of recommendation from influential caring neighbors and my high school records, I was accepted in late August. The University of New Hampshire was notified of my change of plans. I am sure I disappointed the men who initially helped me, but I was once again taking control of my destiny.

2

Duke University

It was a relief to have a new direction. In 1954 I left New England for the first time as Hurricane Carole approached. The train departed South Station for Washington and then went on to Durham, North Carolina. After a long 20-hour trip, I arrived for orientation week and was greeted by upper-class volunteers. Someone put a freshman beanie on my head and I was told always to wear it in public. A mild form of hazing began; my accent had already distinguished me as a Damn Yankee.

We were bused to the quad area and shown to our dorm rooms. Because I was accepted at such a late date, I think rapid accommodations had been made. I was put up in a small room with an army veteran from West Virginia and a Methodist scholarship student from Korea. Because of the cramped living quarters, I avoided this room and when not attending classes, spent most of my time with other dormitory classmates. A few came from New England, but most were from the South. Sharing our background experiences was an education in itself.

The first semester was like my high school days, with a lot of socializing and limited studying. I probably should have followed the example of Fred Chappell and Reynolds Price, both of whom I thought of as bookish nerds. Fred went on to become poet laureate of North Carolina with fourteen books of verse, two volumes of stories, and eight novels to his credit. Reynolds became a Rhodes Scholar and a major southern writer, essayist, and poet. A pretty southern belle in my Spanish class, Elizabeth Hanford went on to become senior class president and May queen; she is known today as Liddy Dole.

During frat week I pledged Delta Tau Delta, thinking that being part of a fraternal family would help guide me to better study habits. But it proved to be only another distraction. The upshot was that I became the "Phantom Pledge" and organized fellow pledges to play foolish pranks on our fraternity leaders. I finished the semester with minimum passing grades.

One of my New England classmates had a car. I, along with a few others, shared expenses back to Massachusetts for the Christmas holidays. My brother had enlisted in the navy and my mother had moved to an apartment in a friend's house in Rockport. I had occasional dates with my nurse-training girlfriend and partied with others home from college. As I recall, we were a bunch of pompous Joe College types boasting of our new experiences.

The trip back to North Carolina was quite different from my first venture into the southland. While waiting for my train, I met my old high school football friend, the super star. He had received a sports scholarship to the University of South Carolina and was heading back in an ROTC uniform. He planned to get a free ride on a troop train going to Camp Lejeune and Parris Island with some of our friends who had gone into the service.

DUKE UNIVERSITY

I thought it was a crazy idea but I went along with it. Although not in uniform I somehow blended in and boarded the train. I guess they mistook me for a new recruit. The ride was a continual party. Beer was passed down the aisles in big galvanized washtubs and we sang every conceivable song. Ninety-nine Bottles of Beer on the Wall to my football friend's version of the Lord's Prayer seemed to be the favorites. You can imagine the unruly musical scene! As we neared the Durham station, I became a little anxious; the train would stop only if there were passengers waiting. It turned out that there were NO passengers to pick up. The train was going fairly slowly, so I jumped off with my luggage. I hit the platform with the forward momentum rolling me along. Outside of a few scrapes, I was unhurt.

I started second semester sharing a large dorm room with another prospective baseball player from Rhode Island. He had relatives on the faculty and had been assigned to one of the best rooms on campus. By coincidence, he also had gone to Vermont Academy, a prestigious prep school, with my old neighborhood artist-coach's son, Malcolm Hibbard. The spacious room was ideal for studying, but I found myself concentrating most of my time on baseball practice. Apparently Mr. Coombs, the retired Duke coach, had scouted me in practice and gave a favorable report, for I became the starting freshman second baseman. The head coach was a Wallace Wade protégé, Clarence "Ace" Parker. A star athlete for Duke, he had gone into professional football and been selected for the Hall of Fame as well as playing baseball with the Brooklyn Dodgers and New York Yankees.

The red clay diamonds of the South were quite different from Cape Ann's ballparks and the heat required some adjustments too. My freshman coach was a hard-driving redneck with a crew cut that would be the envy of any marine recruit sergeant. He said, "Anybody that plays ball for me, chews backy." I had never smoked cigarettes, let alone chewed tobacco, but this being the school that tobacco built, I thought it best to learn. I practiced in my room with a wad of Beechnut chewing tobacco. At first, everything spun around and I would get sick into the wastebasket. Finally, after a week, I confidently placed a large wad in my mouth and went to practice. I must admit the moisture prevented that dry cotton-mouth feeling. All was going well until I got courageous and tried to shift the wad to the other cheek while running. The juice and some of the backy went down my throat. I went into embarrassing violent vomiting spasms right in front of the coach. He just laughed and jokingly said, "That'll teach you, Yankee." The baseball season ended. I had played with some very talented players. One in particular was classified as the fastest 100-yard-dash runner in the world. When he ran to first base, all the scouts in attendance would look at their stopwatches in amazement. He later specialized in track and continued to set records.

The semester also ended, but planning my transport home became complicated. My brother had become very ill with rheumatic fever after completing basic training at the U.S. Naval Training Station in Bainbridge, Maryland; he was in the Bethesda Naval Hospital. It seems the navy had not issued winter gear and the recruits had to train in summer-white uniforms under freezing conditions. John and many others came down with pneumonia and other respiratory diseases. I managed to travel with a group of ball players who lived in the D.C. area and was an overnight guest at the home of one of them. I had also previously made connecting arrangements with another player traveling back to

Massachusetts. We set an appointed time and location to meet after I had seen my brother.

The hospital visit went well and I am sure it was a morale booster for John, but my rendezvous for a ride back home turned out to be a complete fiasco. I arrived at the pickup location at the appointed time and waited and waited. After two hours had passed, it was obvious that I had to hitchhike home. I had a blue-white Duke carryall indicating that I was a student, but I worried that my personal Duke baseball bat might give a different impression. The first car that stopped was driven by a black man in a big finned Cadillac. He was a rhythm and blues disk jockey heading to Philadelphia for his midnight radio show. My brother and I had long been fans of this type of music. My rescuer and I passed the time discussing many of the current songs and our favorite Boston DJ, Symphony Sid.

Just outside Philly I was dropped and soon was picked up by a truck going to the Fulton Fish Market. I had heard about this seafood establishment, but never realized how much activity went on at two o'clock in the morning. The driver had to leave me in lower Manhattan but arranged with another trucker to help me get out of downtown and up near the Merritt Parkway. I was let out on a trucking route adjacent to the parkway and managed to climb over a few fences to get a final hitch into Boston. Luckily a professor from MIT picked me up and brought me right to North Station. It was too early for the next train to Rockport so I made a pillow of my little carryall bag and tried to find comfort on one of the wooden benches. Just as I was falling asleep, one of Boston's finest woke me and said I could not stay there or I would be arrested for vagrancy. I eventually caught the first train out and arrived back in Rockport. Another summer and other adventures were waiting.

My mother's new apartment was in a big house in the woods near the quarries. At one time the area had sustained a thriving granite industry, and many Finns and Swedes had immigrated from the "old country" for employment. I started the summer by returning to the golf club, but my coach advised me to earn more money to offset my college expenses. He worked in the office of the local dropforge company and arranged for me and two other students to be hired on for maintenance work. The hours were from 7:00am to 3:00pm with weekends off, so there was plenty of time for baseball and other summer fun.

I bought my first car from a fellow ballplayer for twenty-five dollars. It was a 1938 baby blue converted funeral car with pull-down velvet shades and other bizarre accoutrements. My so-called steady girlfriend was spending more and more time in Boston with her nursing duties, so we agreed to free each other up from any binding commitments.

The restaurants always hired college students during the busy tourist season. I spent many nights picking up the gang after the restaurants closed and driving them to the night spots on Rocky Neck. This bustling summer artist colony was full of colorful bohemian nightlife. Most of us were underage; it was rare that anyone checked for an ID. If they did, we would flash birth cards with dates that were altered during a Student Government Day event.

How we managed to play and work so hard without getting burned out amazes me today. The job at the foundry was very difficult and dirty. It was an extremely hot summer and we had to apply a black protective paint to the entire plant. It seemed more like tar than paint, and working on the roof over the blast furnaces was almost unbearable. The roof was so hot we had to keep wrapping our boots with damp rags. As the summer progressed, thoughts of returning to Duke became questionable. My grades had not been good and despite my scholarship, the hidden expenses were a problem.

One day, returning home from playing a town team game, I ran into a friend who was attending the Massachusetts Maritime Academy. He was in full uniform heading back after weekend leave and I was in full baseball uniform. It was a fateful encounter. I told him of my Duke concerns and he told me how the Academy was very low cost and there were exciting training cruises to foreign ports. The more he talked, the more interested I became. I realized that here might be an answer to my Duke dilemma, as well as a way of fulfilling my old Naval Academy dreams. He mentioned that the commissioner had a summer home on the Gloucester back shore, and his neighbor was the father of a high school friend of mine.

I quickly contacted my friend's father, who was head of one of the local banks. He had a son at the Maritime Academy and after hearing my concerns felt it was a worthwhile move for me to pursue. Even though the next class had already started he set up an appointment for me.

The commissioner lived in one of the old Victorian mansions overlooking the ocean. The next day I nervously approached and climbed to the large wraparound front porch. I wondered if I was again moving too fast and taking charge of my destiny without giving it full thought. Once again I would probably hurt those who been so helpful. I was greeted by a small man who looked like a character out of a Dickens novel.

I immediately felt as though I was under a microscope. He was full of self-importance. After hearing my background, he put things in motion with one phone call. I was to take care of my affairs and report the following week.

3

Massachusetts Maritime Academy and USS Muliphen AKA-61

It was very difficult telling those who had done so much to help, especially Tink Hale, that I was not going back to Duke. I notified the Ouimet Committee and they agreed to transfer my scholarship funding to the academy. The summer job ended and I was off to Buzzards Bay. With today's highway system the trip only takes a few hours, but in 1955 I spent almost a full day making train connections. I arrived at the little depot alongside the Cape Cod Canal having no idea what to expect.

The MMA of 2008 is nothing like it was in those years. There were no dormitories, school buildings, parade grounds, or athletic fields. Nothing resembled a school of higher education and it certainly did not compare to Duke. I slowly walked a road leading to a large gray training ship named the Charleston. There was one building which I thought must be the admissions hall. I got no response after repeated knocking. Finally some cadets appeared and told me it was only the classroom building, I should report to the ship's quarterdeck. I walked up a gangway and as soon as I set foot on deck and announced myself, the next three years of my life fell into place.

I was told by the officer of the deck to go below and be issued gear and a locker. It was like entering a scene from the twilight zone. Cadets were everywhere performing various duties. The new class year was well into the first month and had already seen the initial hazing onslaught. No one knew who I was or where I came from at this late date. Even the upperclassmen were confused and did not know how to treat me. Some thought I might be a spy for the feared commissioner. Finally the master at arms showed me where to get the necessary clothing and where to find my bunk and locker. There had been a few early dropouts, so space was available. The master at arms was an unkempt old navy chief petty officer who smoked a pipe with spittle drooling onto his chin. He must have thought of me as someone with important connections, for despite his mean reputation I was treated very kindly. Some of my new classmates came forward, tried to explain the system, and told me we were called "youngies."

I settled into the routine of classes and shipboard life and learned to avoid hazing situations. Whenever confronted, I played up the mystique of my late arrival. It was not long before the athletic director sought me out. He was politically well connected and was fully aware of my background. The football season had already begun and he tried to persuade me to join the team. I explained a problem I had with a groin injury, but told him I was willing to join the basketball program and definitely the baseball team when those seasons opened.

In the chance encounter that had led me to Massachusetts Maritime Academy, one of the enticements for me had been the prospect of cruises to foreign ports. During my first year our training ship was to go to the Mediterranean; Spain and Italy were on the itinerary. Before crossing the Atlantic we stopped in

Norfolk, Virginia for a few days. I asked the admiral for a weekend leave so that I could go to Duke and retrieve the personal belongings I had left in storage. To the amazement of the upperclassmen, I was granted this leave. It added to the mystique.

I took a bus to Durham and after checking the contents of my foot locker, realized that none of the books or clothing would fit into my new lifestyle. I went to the baseball field and explained to the coach and some of the players the reason for my career change. I paid a final visit to my fraternity house and dormitory, the chapel, and the library I had seldom used. When I departed for Norfolk, I left real college life behind forever.

On the bus back to Norfolk and the Charleston, I was full of self doubt about the course that I had chosen. *The Brothers Karamazov* eventually took my mind off the subject. During one of the book's violent and bloody passages the bus broadsided a car full of people making an illegal turn. Fiction became reality: blood and bodies lay over the road. We had to wait for another bus. The academy decision had been made, and I would make the most of it.

The cruise was a new adventure and learning experience. We returned into spring and the long-awaited baseball season. After one of the infielders graduated, I became the starting second baseman. MMA played in the Cape Cod League. Most of the teams used college athletes from around the country with older semipro players, so the games were very competitive. It was fun to get off the training ship for a few hours and see the Cape Cod towns at the height of the tourist season.

My first year term came to a close and after only a brief break my second year began. The name "youngie," along with the threat of hazing, was over. Close living on the ship became a little more civilized, but we still had terrible roach-infested food and slept in tiers of four. One of the few socials was the Admiral's Ball, held at the Parker House in Boston. I invited my "on again off again" girlfriend, who was still in nursing school. Neither of us had much experience with alcohol so a lot of misadventures occurred. The relationship went downhill from there.

For me, highlights of the balance of the year were a Caribbean cruise and another baseball season. One of our ports was Houston, Texas. I was one of two cadets chosen to be guests of the Hogg sisters at the Houston Symphony. The sister with the unfortunate name Ima Hogg was a major patron of the arts and had raised a million dollars to lure Leopold Stokowski to conduct Stravinsky's *Firebird*. We were picked up by a limousine and enjoyed a cultural evening with the bejeweled sisters. I later learned that their father, Jim Hogg, was one of the principal land and oil barons of Texas.

After another graduation we became the upper classmen. It was our turn to mete out the hazing and be in complete control, but our year was broken up by the acquisition of a new training ship. The Charleston was going to be condemned. Several of us went to a shipyard in Staten Island to help prepare the new ship. The Bay State, formerly USS Doyen became our hands-on classroom, and New York City became our campus at night. Soon after our return to Buzzards Bay with the new ship, we received clearance for another training cruise. It turned out to be a fiasco filled with constant breakdowns, but we survived. Once back, I was appointed captain of the baseball team. The coach was working on his doctorate at a nearby teachers' college, so many times in his absence I had to be both player and coach. The three-year term ended with finals and the required

Coast Guard exams for merchant marine licenses. I was now twenty-two years old.

USS MULIPHEN AKA-61

After graduating and passing the Coast Guard examinations for third assistant engineer (any tonnage on any ocean), I was commissioned an ensign and required to fulfill a two-year naval obligation. However, our contract had a clause stating that after serving months of active duty one could transfer to the Merchant Marine and remain in the reserves for six years without further active duty. I was assigned to the amphibious cargo ship USS Muliphen AKA-61 She was named after a star in the constellation Canis Major. I quickly learned that the navy and some of its policies did not fit my temperament. I also wanted to make some real money — which I could do on a merchant ship. My time on the Muliphen was spent more or less in limbo, for the officers knew I would be going off active duty in six months.

The ship had just returned to Norfolk from the infamous 1958 invasion of Lebanon. All the Marines had debarked at Morehead City, North Carolina, and the ship was preparing to go into the shipyard. After reporting on board, I was shown to my stateroom. The sign above the door read "Sleepy Hollow"; my new roommates, two young ensigns, greeted me. They happened to be products of the Naval ROTC in college and were very green. At least I had had some experience aboard ship and with close-quarter living. I was given so few assignments, I soon lived up to the Sleepy Hollow name. After morning muster there was nothing for me to do as the division's electrical engineer, so I would go back to bed until the wardroom chimes rang for lunch.

The wardroom gave me a chance to meet my fellow officers and learn a little about the ship.

Apparently the invasion of Lebanon had been an embarrassment. When the ship had arrived the situation was intense, but the Muliphen marine landing force met no opposition after hitting the beaches. In fact, girls in bikinis were sunbathing and vendors tried to sell them food and souvenirs. Children were everywhere begging for candy. The Muliphen's previous history had been quite different; she received two battle stars for participating in the assault and occupation of Iwo Jima and Okinawa. Her nickname was the "Mighty Mule" and her logo was "Many Lands Many Landings." I wonder if this influenced the title of my book. I found out later that she met the fate of too many proud ships when she was scuttled to form an artificial breakwater off Port St. Lucie, Florida.

In attempts to keep me occupied, I was assigned to various shoreside classes. The ship finally went to the shipyard in Newport News, Virginia, and work party activity filled our day. I must that admit most of my "activity" still took place in Sleepy Hollow. Night activity in the city was another matter. One evening, upon entering an after-hours social club, I heard my name called out. To my amazement, a group of Gloucester fishermen were there. Their boat was working the Virginia coast and was in the shipyard for repairs.

Over several weeks I got to know all the local girls the fishermen had befriended. As I've said, my temperament did not fit the navy; I found some of its rules and regulations ridiculous. I was to be officer of the deck over the upcoming Thanksgiving. I learned that several of the girls, especially the ones with children, had no place to go for a holiday dinner. Most of the ship's company was on holiday leave and the skeleton crew that remained on board would never be able to eat the feast that was to be prepared, so I invited anyone who wanted to join us for Thanksgiving dinner. Over thirty mothers and children came and we had a wonderful time. The crew, away from their families at the holiday enjoyed it equally. I thought I was in trouble when summoned to the captain's room the following week, but he said I had made a fine humanitarian gesture - great for morale and public relations for the navy. Maybe my temperament was okay after all?

In that I had the Thanksgiving duty I was given a few days leave and went up to the Army - Navy game with one of the other ensigns. He was an Annapolis graduate and had a new black Chevrolet that carried us up to Philadelphia. As I recall, the weather was bitterly cold and we sat in the end zone drinking brandy to stay warm. The brandy had numbing affects, for I do not remember who won the game. But I do remember celebrating in the hallway of some Philadelphia hotel with a group of us doing the Limbo under a horizontally held floor lamp. Later that night my shipmate and I took a cab to find more excitement. I think the cabbie got the wrong impression for we were taken to an after hours club that turned out to be exclusively for gay men. This revelation brought an immediate sobering end to our festive day.

My brief time in the navy was coming to a close. After my Christmas leave we sailed to Guantanamo Bay and the Caribbean for training exercises. We made enjoyable stops in Puerto Rico and Jamaica before heading back to Norfolk. The Sleepy Hollow routine commenced again, along with being sent to several more five-day schools. Finally I was assigned as refrigeration engineer on a United Fruit Company banana boat, and I could be relieved of active duty.

I think if I deserved any recognition for my brief navy career it would be for achieving the most sack time and for receiving the Thanksgiving Humanitarian Medal.

Part Two:
Life among the Bananas

4

Sailing for the United Fruit Company

In the spring of 1959 I was discharged from active duty. After only two days at home I received a call from my new shipping agent telling me to report to the SS Metapan, one of the United Fruit Company's new banana boats. The ship was docked in Weehawken, New Jersey, and I had only one day to get there and sign on before departing as a Junior Third Refrigeration Engineer.

It might be helpful to share a little company history, and prepare the reader for the new life adventure I was about to undertake. Bananas were unknown in the United States prior to 1870. It was the industrious energy of Minor Keith, a young Brooklyn entrepreneur, that started one of America's largest blue-chip companies. After constructing a railroad in Costa Rica, he planted bananas on the land easements on either side of the tracks. Keith would do anything to advance his own interests, even to marrying the daughter of the Costa Rican president. This calculated move paid off and he became known as the uncrowned king of Central America. The banana venture flourished. With the railroad completed it was economically feasible to transport the bananas to markets in the United

States and Europe. By the turn of the century Americans were consuming 16 million bunches a year. Keith teamed up with a Cape Cod sailor, Captain Lorenzo Baker, and a Boston business man, Andrew Preston. They raised money to found the Boston Fruit Company. In 1899 it merged with the United Fruit Company to become the largest banana company in the world, with plantations throughout Central America. They owned and leased a vast fleet of steamships, and hundreds of miles of railroads linking the plantations with ports. Throughout the early 1900s their empire grew through political dictatorship and favoritism. Much has been written about the company known as La Frutera - or unfavorably by many as el Pulpo, the Octopus. It gained virtual control of all means of transport and communication in these countries; its strong CIA connections with the Eisenhower administration made it an ever more powerful influence in this part of the world. Yet the company also built houses, schools, hospitals, and research labs to conquer tropical diseases. When I joined the company, the unions were becoming stronger with the influence of leaders such as Che Guevara.

I reported on board the twin-screw Metapan and was shown to a stateroom that made Sleepy Hollow looked like something out of shantytown. My steward was a tall black man dressed in a starched white uniform. He pointed out a carafe of ice water and fruit in the small refrigerator. The bulkheads were richly paneled and there was only one large bunk. I was shown the location of the lavish dining room and told I had the 8 to 12 watches (am and pm) with a senior refrigerator engineer. We departed on schedule and headed for what I thought was to be Honduras.

The United Fruit Company's banana boats, also known as the Great White Fleet, loaded in ports on both coasts of Central America, as well as in Guayaquil, Ecuador. Usually product loaded on the east coast of Panama and Honduras went to New Orleans, Charleston or New York. West coast product went to San Francisco or Seattle. Along with its perishable cargo, the ships carried twelve passengers.

The nature of the cargo meant that the ships usually went directly to the banana ports. On this particular trip we were mysteriously diverted to Norfolk to load frozen meat - at least that is what I was told. (Our ultimate destination was the navy base at Guantanamo, Cuba.) Fidel Castro had recently come to power and had taken control from the corrupt Batista organization. He had also expropriated all Cuban holdings of United Fruit.

By coincidence we tied up forward of my former navy ship. Some of the line handlers were from my duty section, and they were some surprised to see me. My transition from navy to merchant marine in only a week became really apparent when I invited them up to my stateroom. They stared with envy. It was quite a change from Sleepy Hollow, where I had shared quarters with two other junior officers.

The meat was loaded at night. I suspect guns and ammunition were also included to support a future clandestine attack on Fidel. But what did a junior engineer know?

After leaving Cuba, my suspicions grew as a result of the unexpected suicide of the chief engineer. He was one of the senior engineers in the company and a much respected rear admiral in the naval reserves. The connection of United Fruit and the CIA is well documented. I suspect financing and supporting revolutions to maintain power might have overwhelmed him. The chief's death was a true engineering feat. He was right on schedule in his routine of yelling down to the engine room at midnight, "Is everything all right, junior? Have a good night." After I waved an okay, he retired to his room. Sometime during my midnight to 4:00am watch he had gone into the shower, sealed the door with tape, and fired off a CO_2 bottle into his mouth. On arrival in Puerto Cortez the chief's body was removed from refrigerated storage and flown back to the States.

Memories of my first banana port are always enhanced when I hear Harry Belafonte's *Day-O* song. The ship came into port on my night watch and it wasn't until I stepped out on deck after midnight that my senses became fully activated. The heat and humidity were oppressive and the smells emanating from the low-lying jungle were like nothing I had ever experienced; swamp gas coming out of an open furnace would be close. The dock was an extension of a railroad track that began in the interior jungle plantations. In those days the banana bunches, which contained around fifteen hands, were cut by machetes and dipped into large chemical vats, then loaded on the flat-bed railway cars. After arrival on the docks, the banana bunches were put on the shoulders of barebacked native longshoremen and one by one placed on the ship's conveyor belts. Occasionally a painful cry would ring out as a loader's shoulder erupted from a poisonous snake bite. It is my understanding that bananas are now graded and boxed for pallet loading to the refrigerated cargo hold. This procedure is not as romantic as Harry's song and the "tallyman" is no longer needed to count the number of bunches loaded by the poor natives.

Despite the jungle heat and smells, I could not resist going into town. I was told Mamacita's was the most popular cantina. After clearing the armed guards at the dock gate, I went down the shanty-lined dirt Main Street. Even though it was late at night, the street was filled with children, dogs, chickens, pigs, vendors, and all kinds of activity. After all, the ship was in, and despite the squalor it was almost festive. Mamacita's neon lights and Spanish music filled the night. I enjoyed a few cool cervezas (beers) and enjoyed a few dances with the "local" girls. One in particular interested me and I hoped to see her next time we came back.

Loading continued through the night and we departed in the morning. I was one of three refrigerator engineers whose job it was to keep the bananas at around 52 degrees so they would not ripen before getting back to the States. Life on board was a great experience. As an officer, I ate with the passengers. The food was excellent and presented as though in a five-star restaurant. The diverse backgrounds of the passengers and my fellow shipmates also made the voyages true learning experience. The passengers were usually adventurous types looking for a different escape. They had to have an open travel schedule, for sometimes strange diversions occurred.

Once because of weather-related harvesting problems in California and Mexico, a tomato shortage occurred. The produce giants, known as Tomato Kings, became desperate and sought any possible supply solution. We ceased loading bananas and went to Haiti, where apparently tomatoes were plentiful. The powers-to- be always sent us to where the biggest buck could be made, despite the dangers. Haiti at that time was under the dictatorship of "Papa Doc" Duvalier. I remember being on watch when we picked up the pilot and proceeded to the dock. Armed soldiers were stationed on the bridge and in the engine room. Behind the first engineer and me were four soldiers with rifles pointed at our heads who scrutinized our every move. I guess they were making sure we were only coming for tomatoes. Loading went without incident and we were off to New York. Our arrival was like the return of the "Big U" (SS United States); the dock was filled with cheering, dancing Tomato Kings. We had brought home the gold. Reefer trucks and vans of all sizes were in position to load and speed off to market. Impatient vendors would push aside longshoremen, open crates as soon as they came off the conveyors, kiss and hold up tomatoes like trophies. I never saw such passion for produce except perhaps banana feeding time in the gorilla cage at the Bronx Zoo.

5

Shipboard Encounters and Puerto Cortez Revisited

The saying aboard ship was, "The bananas are the guests and the passengers the pests." A pretty young woman from Canada came on board for one of our trips to Honduras. She was by no means a pest, just a nice single girl looking to find herself. Well, she found me and a little shipboard romance started up. Because I wasn't allowed in the passenger area, we had to come up with a rendezvous strategy. I got off watch at midnight but she usually fell asleep before then. Coordinating our time schedules was quickly solved with typical Massachusetts Maritime Academy ingenuity. Her cabin was off the lifeboat deck and there was a handy porthole by her bunk. I told her to tie a string to her toe and dangle it out the porthole. After midnight I would come by and jiggle the string so we could rendezvous in my cabin. This worked fine for a few nights until some of the crew caught on. They jiggled the poor girl's toe at all kinds of odd hours, so we had to put an end to this novel nocturnal encounter. When the ship returned to New York, we enjoyed a final night dining at a German restaurant in the Yorkville section of upper Manhattan. The goodbye was a little sad, but I must say it was a satisfying ending. She had "found herself" and could return to Canada fulfilled.

I was now sailing as third engineer and noticed that people who chose to book passage on our ship were really trying to "get away from it all". Once it was Marilyn Monroe's private secretary after the star's suicide or assassination. A black-haired statuesque beauty, she came aboard with a male escort. All of us on the ship immediately fantasized about a shipboard romance with her. I used to watch her walk the deck, seemingly lost in sad moments. After a few days at sea, I mustered up the courage to talk to her. After the usual chitchat she broke down and told me she needed to get away. I think it was for more than emotional reasons as I found out later that frightening questions still surround the tragedy. I must have had a calming effect, for she became curious about my work and wanted to know what I did when we reached port.

The particular banana port we reached I think was Armuelles, Panama, for we were on the west coast run. It was your typical jungle setting, with a jutting dock and railroad track. This port was a little more upscale than others, for in the distance were pristine white United Fruit buildings that housed the country club, hospital, school, and living quarters for resident employees. It was a startling contrast to the dock area. The secretary asked if she could go ashore when I got off watch to see the night life. When I got off at midnight she was waiting. "I want to see where you go", she said. That being the other side of the tracks and not the country club, I asked her, "Are you sure you really want to go there?" She replied with an emphatic "Yes".

So off we went in the steamy night, leaving the bustling banana loading dock behind. Harry Belafonte was right on: "Work all night for a bottle of rum." Across the tracks, life was bustling to a different beat. The cantinas were brightly lit and Latin music filled the air. The locals and *putas* (aka whores) were everywhere, for a ship was in port. Cerveza and rum flowed and sweating bodies rhythmically danced. Like Dorothy in Oz she loved the sudden excitement. We sat at a table just taking it all in until a khaki-clad soldier toting a submachine gun came over and asked for her "health papers". I tried to explain that she was a passenger on the ship, not a *puta*, but I was not getting my message across and he was going to take her away. Finally I hailed a Puerto Rican oiler from the ship; he explained in far better Spanish and all was forgiven. Cerveza and rum flowed again to everyone's delight. I do mean everyone, for the registered senoritas thought some serious competition had come to town. Being mistaken for a *puta* made the secretary's day and restored whatever femininity she had lost or questioned. Sorry, but the rest of the trip was uneventful.

PUERTO CORTEZ REVISITED

Once again we returned to a steamy banana port in Honduras. The ship was now on a weekly run between New Orleans and Puerto Cortez. As a young marine engineer, I found the diverse cultures stimulating and often challenging. The treatment of the young whores at Mamacita's was difficult to comprehend unless you really experience the country's poverty and the dominance of the Catholic Church. If an unmarried girl became pregnant, she was thrown out on the street and left on her own. The harbor was known as the Sea of Fetuses.

On one of these banana loading trips, I tried to bring a little joy to those I called prisoners. The girls at Mamacita's were confined to small rooms like cells and could never leave the compound. Mamacita herself was a tiny wizened woman of mixed Indian and Spanish blood known as a Mestizo. She ruled the house of ill repute with an iron fist. Her helper Leo was aptly named, for he had a frightening appearance - a cross between the hunchback of Notre Dame, a Sumo wrestler, and a jungle cat. This look, coupled with his questionable intelligence, really provided the control.

One day we arrived ahead of schedule. It was a typical 100-degree, 100-percent-humidity afternoon. The temperatures were still unbearable. After many trips, I had made friends with Lillian, the girl I met on my first trip. A nice relationship had developed and I always brought back little gifts from New Orleans for her, Mamacita, and Leo. This proved very helpful, for I usually had extra overnight privileges and, in general, a trustful feelings from all of them. This particular afternoon, as I walked along the dirt road lined with tin shacks, yelling children, barking dogs, and desperate vendors trying to sell fly-covered goods, I had a humane fun-filled thought; why not ask Mamacita if I could take all the girls to the beach. After all, nothing really happened in the heat of the day in her cantina, and if I was willing to pay, what could be the problem? The problem was Leo. The girls being entrusted to me and out of his control was something he could not understand, but businesswoman Mamacita immediately saw the value of this outing. Money for a slow afternoon, and probably a good time for the girls, would ease the tensions that always existed in such tight living conditions. She managed to persuade Leo, and with their blessing my twelve disciples and I marched off to La Playa. Before we left there was a lot of discussion about what to wear, for the women really had no suitable bathing suits.

Makeshift shorts and tee shirts worked for everyone but Lillian. She would not go unless she had a proper bathing suit. Finally, majority ruled - along with my promise to buy her one in New Orleans.

The beach outing was a great success. The girl's shrieks of "Cuidado Tibron, Tibron" saved me from a circling shark and added a few words to my growing Spanish vocabulary. The procession back through the poor thronging natives was like Jesus leading his faithful followers. Word spread through the port town that a young engineer off the banana boat had taken Mamacita's *putas* to La Playa. There were no hosannas, but I certainly felt like a "hero of the people". Even Leo, upon my return, grunted through a toothless grin and gave me a full embrace. That night the girls sang and danced and "performed" like never before. Mamacita was ecstatic.

We always felt relief and joy upon arrival in New Orleans. Coming through the heavy ship traffic of the Mississippi River called for skillful piloting. The engine room of a twin-screw steam turbine ship constantly had to respond to bridge orders. Usually I was on one throttle and the first engineer, if he was sober, on the other. Many times I bobbed and weaved alone between answering the telegraph bells and controlling the throttles. "Shut Down Engines" was a welcome call. "New Orleans, New Orleans, City of Dreams". Truly. Fine food, jazz, French and Cajun culture, Bourbon Street, Mardi Gras, all cradled in the arm of the mighty Mississippi. Going ashore was always an adventure.

On this particular occasion the day's priority was going shopping at the best store in town, Maison Blanc, for the promised bathing suit. The lure of Bourbon Street would wait. It was not my custom to shop in the women's department, especially for a bathing suit. So I just pointed to a clerk of similar size and said, "I'd like to buy a bathing suit to fit her, and I want the best." I could hear giggles from the various clerks, but a colorful pink two-piece Rose Marie was quickly selected and tastefully boxed for a very deprived young girl in Honduras. The box became my closely held escort that night. I had dinner at Brennan's, did some barhopping, and staggered back to the ship. The unloading of bananas was proceeding when one of the longshoremen, noticing the nicely wrapped box, yelled out, "Hey mate, something for your mother?" Little did he know, or could he ever understand, the purpose of the contents. After another quick turnaround, we headed back down the river to the open sea.

The calm trips to and from Cortez were uneventful. The weather was hot, but usually accompanied by a cool breeze until we neared the coast. The high humidity and smell of the jungle became prevalent as we maneuvered into port. Waiting for us were the usual trainloads of bananas, native longshoremen, and the ubiquitous soldiers with submachine guns. It was a little after midnight when I arrived at Mamacita's cantina. Everything was in full swing: Mexican cowboy music, sweating couples dancing, tables strewn with bottles of cerveza. Mamacita and Leo were waiting with toothless grins for my little gifts from New Orleans.

There was added excitement in the air when the girls saw the pretty box. But I must say, I almost didn't get past the soldiers at the dock gate. Between the gifts and a ticking bulge in my shirt pocket, I thought I was headed for the calaboose. I tried to explain that the ticking bulge was from my alarm clock, for I planned to spend the night with Lillian. (I told you I had special privileges at Mamacita's.) The soldiers, guns pointed, had me surrounded. My limited Spanish was no help at all. It was getting to a very critical moment, when one of the Puerto Rican oilers on the ship came by. I explained the box and ticking bulge to him, and he in turn translated to the soldiers. Great laughter and backslapping followed, for they remembered me from the puta beach party. Word spread fast and before I reached the cantina, it seemed like a hundred kids were skipping along beside me, chanting "Man with the Tick Tock. Man with the Tick Tock."

Later that night, after the cantina had closed, the girls gathered around Lillian as she opened her package from Maison Blanc. The only fancy or pretty material goods these girls ever saw were in catalogues. When the Rose Marie emerged from the box, sighs and cries were heard through the night. The bathing suit proved totally satisfactory but it would never be worn. It was immediately nailed up on the wall and looked upon like a religious icon or some great work of art. I wonder if on some barrio wall in Puerto Cortez this objet d'art still hangs; I have never had the opportunity to return.

6

Panama Canal and Other Ports

We went through the Panama Canal several times en route to Guayaquil (Ecuador), Golfito (Costa Rica), Puerto Armuelles (Panama), and up to San Francisco and Seattle. Transiting the canal is a fascinating experience. Every movement through the locks is critical. Once we lost power and tied up the canal for almost a day. After failing to resolve the situation, we were towed into Lake Gatun to allow the backed-up shipping traffic to resume. We finally found a vacuum leak in the turbine casing after stripping off the asbestos lining; an engineering turbine specialist from General Electric was flown down with the needed parts. Needless to say, this episode was a major embarrassment to all connected with the ship. As I recall, the shipment of bananas bound for New York had unfortunately ripened owing to the delay. The radio operator made many calls to schools and hospitals in the canal area and as far away as Charleston, South Carolina, offering free perfectly good bananas, but there were not enough responses. We had to dump our cargo off the Virginia coast. It made a sea of yellow as far as the eye could see.

The next trip through the canal was exciting as always, but uneventful. Because of crop damage caused by the wind, we had to skip the Panamanian plantations and go to Ecuador. To reach Guayaquil you have to travel up the Guayas River. The current is so swift that we had to anchor away from the city dock and load the ship from barges; the engines had to run at slow speed ahead to avoid anchor dragging. One particular night I went ashore alone. Several natives were already in the boat, all clothed in black. I was immediately told to stay low and not look up. The boat started heading downstream away from the public dock. My protests were met by, "Just stay down and everything will be all right." I had no choice but to comply. After about thirty minutes I heard the engine slow down and I took a quick peek despite the warnings. We were heading into a thick grove of riverbank trees where signals flashed from waiting compatriots. Someone raised a canvas and boxes were unloaded to the shore side rendezvous. I kept silent and down, not knowing if I was part of an exchange of arms or drugs. The transactions took only a few minutes, but to me they seemed like hours. Later I was told that I was to be bartered or held for ransom if the smuggling adventure ran into problems. Isn't it nice to be needed!

We made several trips to San Francisco and Seattle. I particularly liked going to San Francisco. I was very interested in the Beat Poet movement, and when in New York I used to frequent the bars in Greenwich Village. I could find some of the same poets, writers, painters, and musicians in the North Beach section of San Francisco. Lawrence Ferlingetti's City Lights Bookstore was a popular literary Mecca and was helpful in getting controversial poets such as Allen Ginsberg published. I remember meeting the colorful Patrick Shamus O'Sullivan in a North Beach bar, selling new poems for 25 cents a mimeographed page. Only a few months earlier I had seen him in the Village dressed in a flowing green cape and boasting of how he had led the city's Saint Patrick's Day parade on a horse painted Kelly green. The beatniks piqued my interest; for years I remained on the fringe of their movement and met many of their entertainers - Bob Dylan, Bill Crosby, and Phyllis Diller, to name a few.

I thoroughly enjoyed Nob Hill and the cable cars, as well as the great restaurants and sophistication of San Francisco. We usually unloaded half our cargo, then traveled up the coast to Seattle for the final discharge. On one trip while I was on watch, we were off the coast of Washington going full steam ahead. Suddenly a telegraph call "Full Astern" came from the bridge. On a twin-screw ship it takes time to make this adjustment. Just as we were starting to slow down, there was a collision. We had hit a large whale. There was no apparent damage to the ship, but we proceeded with caution through Puget Sound. The fate of the whale was unfortunate but at least we had not hit another vessel or lost any lives. That engine room experience made me reflect on how dangerous and chaotic World War II convoy maneuvers must have been. My memories of Seattle are vague except that we were there during preparations for the upcoming world's fair. The tall space needle that was erected stands today as a symbol of the city, like the arch in St. Louis. I recall enjoying smoked salmon at an open market. Fishmongers threw the fish back and forth as if at a sporting event. My salmon order was casually served on a newspaper and I walked to a nearby park bench to devour every tasty bite.

By coincidence, I ran into a former Gloucester classmate, now an engineer with Boeing Aircraft. I think the whole economy of the city relied on Boeing. This chance meeting in a wine bar included my first experience with a Thunderbird Special. This concoction of cheap Thunderbird wine and ginger ale was becoming very popular, but it certainly did not please my taste, which had been cultivated for scotch. I was never on watch during our departures from Seattle, so I could observe the beauty of the surrounding area as we went out through Puget Sound.

SHIPMATE ENCOUNTERS

It was on one these West Coast trips that I had a run-in with the second engineer. We had both been on the ship for almost nine months and he was developing some strange mannerisms. At first he thought he was being poisoned and refused to eat in the dining room. He would take his food up to one of the top decks and feed the sea gulls. Only after the gulls showed no signs of distress would he eat or drink. Then he began accusing me of leaving the engine room in unacceptable condition for his watch. His paranoia got progressively worse. Thinking I might reason with him I made the mistake of going to his stateroom one night. A stateroom is a man's private sanctuary with virtually full maritime law protection. After letting me in, he went berserk and started pulling pages off a calendar on the bulkhead and screaming out the months that he had been aboard. He then took a fire axe and pressed it to my throat. His ranting about being away from family continued and in the confusion it became obvious that he was mistaking me for one of his sons. I remained very still during the encounter and he finally ran down emotionally. The axe dropped as he sobbingly crumpled into the fetal position. I opened the door to find the captain, the chief engineer and other fellow officers waiting helplessly. The second engineer was restrained and sedated. Afterward, he made sincere apologies. I heard later that a similar event occurred on another ship and that he was taken off in Seattle in a straitjacket. His was an isolated case. Most of my shipmates were fun to sail with and we shared some memorable times.

One of the chief engineers was known to be very tough on young maritime graduates; it was best to just do your job well and stay out of his way. The ship was unloading in Mobile, Alabama where Front Street goes right down to the docks. Like most waterfront streets it is lined with a series of infamous barrooms. It was there in Joe Palooka's that I unfortunately encountered the chief. He was a big, gruff, Nordic type and was squatting on a stool. The bar was crowded and all the stools were taken, so I stood behind him hoping he would not notice me. I signaled for a scotch and as I reached in to pick it up, I guess I nudged him too hard. His custom-made fedora fell off as the stool spun and he toppled onto the floor. There was a deep silence throughout the bar, for everyone knew his fury. He rose up, restored his fedora to its proper place, and in a stentorian voice bellowed, "It took a goddam junior engineer to knock me on my arse. The drinks are on me." I never mentioned this episode back on the ship, but I think it went down in the annals of United Fruit legends.

I have many shipmate stories I could share, but let me recount just one more. As I reported earlier, one of the first engineers with whom I sailed had a drinking problem. When maneuvering in and out of port, he was supposed to help me man the throttles. Since this seldom happened, it became a challenge to see how well I could respond to calls from the bridge. I think he felt a little guilty, because one time after tying up in New York, he invited the other young third engineer and me out to his Staten Island luxury apartment to meet his wife and have dinner. His directions from the ferry were a little vague, so the other engineer and I came up with a brilliant scheme. As we walked from the landing up winding streets to his apartment, we left a trail of red pistachio nuts. The evening went well. His very attractive wife produced a gourmet meal. The apartment was on the twentieth floor and looked out on the Manhattan skyline. As expected, we all drank too much. During our goodbyes we assured the couple we could find our way back. As we stepped out into the night, we noticed that pigeons or some critters had eaten all our nuts. The best-laid plans of mice and men! Following the sounds of the ferry, we finally staggered into the terminal and boarded for the crossing back to New York. It might have been an apparition, but I think I saw a tall woman in the harbor holding up a torch as a salute to our trailblazing adventure.

Part Three:
Beginning Again

7

Turning the Page

I was home on summer vacation and planned to report to a new ship in September, but life takes strange twists. I ran into a young woman I had known before entering the academy. Pat had a three year-old daughter and had recently divorced. We seemed to enjoy each other's company. When it was time for me to return to New York for another ship assignment, she rode down with me. The plan was for Pat to drive my car back and we would get together over the Christmas holidays. On the way to New York, I, at twenty-six years of age, impulsively decided to halt my nomadic life and settle down. I quit United Fruit, and we drove back in quiet contemplation as to what would happen next.

Over the next months, Pat and I decided to get married. We made arrangements with a shipmate who had also quit the company and was living in Longmeadow, Massachusetts. He and his wife agreed to stand up for us. The ceremony was performed in the kitchen of a justice of the peace, with barking dogs providing background music. My shipmate's boss arranged an elegant private wedding dinner at the Longmeadow Country Club. Ironically, that night Pat and I drove to New York City for a short honeymoon. Even on our wedding day anxiety and nervousness led to the beginning of a strained relationship. The tension grew as we reached the Big Apple. I was very interested in finances and in my naiveté thought a visit to the New York Stock Exchange would be exciting. In retrospect, it was not the most romantic place to take a bride. The tension erupted into crying and shouting. In keeping with my youthful innocence and lack of experience with women, I thought the logical solution would be a visit to the United Nations. After all, wasn't that where countries peacefully resolved their problems? I was wrong again. Being an old baseball player, I knew I had struck out. The honeymoon was cut short and we headed back to Massachusetts. Before we left New York we had dinner at O'Henry's in Greenwich Village and Jack Lemmon happened to come in and pass our table. A touch of celebrity life created enough excitement to fill the personal void.

SHORESIDE AND BACK TO SEA

Pat was teaching and owned a home in Ipswich, Massachusetts from her previous marriage. We settled in there and after a few job interviews I began a training program for safety engineering with a major casualty insurance company. During this time I thought the proper thing to do was adopt her daughter, Kimberly. Soon afterward I was assigned by the company to Atlanta, Georgia. I had recently passed the National Board of Examinations test and was now certified as a boiler and pressure-vessel examiner. We had our household goods packed and shipped. The company even purchased our house in order to speed the transition.

TURNING THE PAGE

We arrived in Atlanta on a hot day shortly before the July Fourth weekend. We used a motel as a base of operation until our furniture came and we could locate a rental house. The company was getting a little upset at paying all this expense. I was told on the holiday to go out to inspect a boiler explosion at a chicken processing plant. The operation was a state of the art predecessor to the Perdue and Tyson operations of today. After inspecting the damage and touring the plant, I had an impressive interview with the owner. Despite looking like a redneck farmer, he was way ahead of his time and proudly told me that everything was processed without waste.

When I returned to the motel, I learned that all our furniture had been damaged when the truck went under a low bridge. Luckily the moving company was one of our insured customers so I was given clearance to go out and replace what we needed. Within the next few days we found a house to rent and a furniture store that filled our needs. The store owners were very helpful in welcoming us to the area and we formed an immediate friendship. Along with the furniture store, they were beginning to stock a line of western riding equipment and apparel to fit their interest in horses. We soon became interested in horses as well, and bought a few inexpensive pleasure horses. Twilight and weekend family rides with our new friends were very enjoyable. At the time, the state was clearing and preparing for the interstate beltways around Atlanta; these dirt roads made great riding trails. When I drive through or around Atlanta today, I cannot believe that these highways were our old trails.

I must say that my dealings with horses were as innocent as my dealings with marriage - probably a good indicator of how crazy things were starting to get. We had acquired an uncontrollable black stallion from a farmer because the price was right. Our horses were kept in a pasture with a neighbor's horses. I had no idea that a stallion had to be boarded separately until there was a call from the Georgia state police. Prince, our stallion, was leading six mares down the highway. I was told to get up there and corral them back or else. Once Prince was restrained, the others meekly followed him back to the pasture.

My safety inspection job covered five southern states. I had a company car and enjoyed the work, but the wages were meager. A small stock brokerage firm in my old hometown of Rockport was looking to expand. Once again I acted impulsively and quit the insurance company. We sold all the horses except for Prince, packed our belongings, and towed a U-Haul back to Massachusetts. It was in the middle of a New England winter and we arrived in a blinding snowstorm. After staying briefly with family, we rented a small house. I was emphatically told by my in-laws that it was not practical to keep Prince, so he was given to the stable owner in lieu of the boarding fee. I started training to be a stock broker and Pat obtained a temporary teaching position.

The next period in my life is rather foggy. My marriage was breaking down and I was having difficulty adding to our joint income on $60 a week plus commissions. The commissions were slow in coming because I was not cut out for cold canvassing. Furthermore, I did not believe in the risky over-the-counter stocks we were trying to sell. At some point we moved to a rental house in Rockport, but I don't think either one of us was acting rationally, especially with a young adopted daughter involved. We finally agreed that I should go back to sea and Pat would find a permanent teaching position away from the area. Maybe being apart would put things in better perspective.

TURNING THE PAGE

I signed up with the marine engineer's union in New York and soon got a relief engineering position on the passenger ship *SS America*. What a difference from the twelve-passenger banana boats! The New York to Southampton (England) run was filled with new experiences. One of my jobs was to tend the saltwater evaporators and make sure they provided enough fresh water for the thousands of crew and passengers on board. I also had to regularly test the watertight doors throughout the ship. I especially enjoyed performing these tests in the first-class area, where I could see how the other half lived.

After returning to New York, I signed up and waited around the union hall for another ship. Listening to the sea stories and learning about the backgrounds of the older merchant mariners was an education in itself. WWII encounters with German U-boats, fearful trips on the Murmansk run, and all the South Pacific invasions seemed to be the popular topics of conversation. It was always a "can you top this" atmosphere. Because I was amenable to doing temporary relief work and was not particular about what kind of ship or what kind of routing, I obtained a third engineer's job with U.S. Lines in just a few days. The ship made what they called the "Whiskey Run". We sailed to Bremerhaven, Rotterdam and Antwerp to unload various cargos. We then went up around northern England into Glasgow and Liverpool to load whiskey for the Boston and New York markets. While in Liverpool, I recall seeing billboards and flyers announcing a popular new band. The local young people were all excited, so I took in one of the performances. They later became known as the Beatles.

On arrival in Boston, I witnessed how the so-called Mafia controlled the docks. Apparently by unwritten agreement 10 percent of the cargo would be stolen; no work stoppages would occur and no one would be hurt. One of the young third mates supervising the unloading of the whiskey and the European cars became too diligent and was shot to death. We all learned to mind our business in some of these areas. I made another relief trip on the *America* after completing the Whiskey Run and scheduled my time to spend the holidays in Gloucester. It was during a gift-bearing Christmas morning visit to my in-laws to see my estranged wife and daughter that a major argument erupted. The marriage was obviously beyond saving.

I returned to New York and signed onto a Moore McCormack ship going to South America. The long trip gave me time to accept the situation and do some serious reflecting. I had to let go and get on with my life. The SS *Mor Mac Hawk* was a well-maintained ship and the Brazilian ports of Belem, Forteleza, Recife and naturally Rio de Janeiro were new and exciting. I had an educational awakening in Recife after unloading Food for Peace containers from the States, I noticed communist-controlled dock workers placing "USSR" stickers over USA. As you can see, life on the docks was filled with more than bustling commercial activity.

Upon arrival in Rio, we had to anchor out in the harbor because a longshoreman's strike had started over *carga vergona*. This was shame cargo, such as toilet paper and sanitary napkins, and the men wanted extra compensation. The strike lasted for over thirty days, so I had a month of unexpected travel pleasures. Life in Brazil was especially exciting in the 60s. The *cruizero,* their dollar, was going crazy with inflation. Things were cheap if you had American dollars. I enjoyed this longshoreman's tie-up completely. Coffee bars, theater, racetracks, colorful nightlife, and Copacabana Beach provided endless amusement.

TURNING THE PAGE

One day I ventured to the beach. Our ship was still anchored out in the harbor, so the trip required a boat shuttle and a five mile bus ride. I saw a nice-looking family group and asked them to watch my belongings while I took a dip. Girls from Ipenema and the cross-currents must have disoriented me. Upon returning I could not find the family gathering or my belongings. There I stood wearing only bathing trunks on a beach in a foreign country. No papers! No money! Nothing! What to do? Even though Portuguese was the language of Brazil, I started yelling "ladron... ladron," which I thought meant thief in Spanish. No results, no one cared!!

Finally, collecting my thoughts, I looked around and noticed a coastal patrol boat. I waded out as far as possible to get attention. The crew became aware of a problem and pointed to their headquarters at the far end of the beach. Desperate, I trekked to the patrol station a mile or so away, never even glancing at the Girls from Ipenema. That tells you something about my plight. Upon arrival at the headquarters, I tried to explain my situation in mixed Spanish and Portuguese. The station was some kind of international Coast Guard operation and luckily the officer in charge was from Canada. After a few laughs over my dilemma, he radioed for his personal Chris-Craft and I was ferried back. I spent the next day at the U.S. embassy trying to replicate my Z-card information (the merchant mariner's passport) and other data in order to be a person again. To this day I wonder who holds my identity in Brazil.

Outside of adventurous and pleasurable activities, I recall seeing the entire Russian whaling fleet arrive one day after having been on the Antarctic fishing grounds for over six months. Not having the freedom we had, they went ashore in numbered groups with an armed guard. It must have been frustrating after the long confinement on their whaling voyage. Passing by them on the shuttle boat or meeting them on the dock, we would exchange teasing greetings. "F--- you, Russkie!" They would reply, "F--- you, Ameriskie!" It was all in fun despite the language difficulties; waves, handshakes, and hearty laughter were always present. Before heading back to New York, the ship went to Porto Allegro. It was here that I saw real horse and cattle country. The normal two-month trip took more than three months. I was ready to return to Gloucester and ready to start a new phase of my life.

In Gloucester I stayed briefly with my mother, who was more than glad to see her wayward son. After a year and a half, the marriage was over and it was agreed that I would go to Georgia for a quick divorce. Just as I was starting off, I was stopped by a Massachusetts state trooper for speeding. It was 5:00am. No one else was on the road and I was feeling free. The officer turned out to be an acquaintance from Gloucester, and when I told him I was speeding to get a divorce, he just laughed and waved me on with a big good luck greeting. After the divorce procedure, I visited some of our old friends in Atlanta and drove by the pasture and rental house. Another part of my life had come to a close.

During the summer in Gloucester, I resumed contact with a fellow graduate of the maritime academy. A brilliant inventor type, he had developed some electronic methods to revolutionize the fishing industry. We had met on previous occasions in New York and discussed teaming up to form a new corporation. Now we put together several venture capital proposals to get start-up money for his new fishing concepts. Interest was great, but we were not successful; nor did a trip to Nova Scotia to get Canadian government backing succeed. Our experience in trying to launch a new venture added to my education in the school of life.

This must have been my summer of turning points, because I met a very interesting divorcee with three children. She was having great difficulty adjusting to the fact that her husband had left her for another woman. We soon formed a relationship, as I wanted to be close by to help her through her situation.

The fishing venture was going nowhere, so instead of going back to New York I worked out of Boston, taking night relief engineering jobs throughout New England. When a ship was in port, the Coast Guard required that a licensed officer be on board. It was my job to report to a ship that had arrived to discharge or load cargo (or in the case of tankers, pump out fuel) and relieve the regular engineer at night. I did this work for almost a year.

My woman friend and I were developing a close friendship but decided to take a break and see where the relationship was going. She recognized the reality of the situation, telling me that I was still young and didn't need to be saddled with another man's children. I felt terrible leaving, but I knew a break was best. I left, saying without really meaning it, "I have places to go and people to see."

I returned to the union hall in New York and it wasn't long before I got another relief engineering position on the SS *Fairland* going to Puerto Rico. The Sea Land Shipping Company was introducing a new container concept to reduce pilfering and to speed the cargo-handling operation. Hundreds of 18-wheelers would arrive at the terminal in Elizabeth, New Jersey, and have their containerized trailers lifted off by special gantries. They would then be properly placed and secured aboard specially designed ships. Everyone thought the trucking mogul Malcolm McLean was crazy to have invested so much in this concept, but he was proven right and it is now the preferred method of transporting goods. I was fortunate to have a small role in these historic trial runs.

Upon my return from Puerto Rico I continued with night engineering jobs around the New York and Brooklyn waterfront. The current ships would serve as my hotel room at night and the union hall as my base of operation during the day. New York was a wonderfully diverse cultural playground and I thoroughly digested all that was offered. After a few weeks, I got a relief third engineering job on an oil tanker going to Corpus Christi, Texas. It was my first time sailing as engineer on a turbo electric drive tanker. All my other experience had been on steam turbines, but this engine crew was very well trained and helped me learn the engine room procedure. Once again the time away helped me reflect on the direction of my life, but I wondered whether running off to sea would continue be the correct answer.

Arriving in Corpus Christi, I was relieved by the regular third engineer. I stayed at one of the old hotels until I could get a ship back to the East Coast. There wasn't much activity at the union hall in Corpus. I stayed about a week before realizing that I would have to go to busy Houston for possible employment. The next day I departed by bus for Houston. It didn't take long to get a ship going back to the East Coast. The only problem was that the job was for a second engineer on another tanker. I had upgraded my merchant marine license to second after putting enough sea time in with United Fruit, but I had never had any experience in this position.

Reporting to the chief at an oil refinery upriver near Baton Rouge, I made my case clear. He was just glad to have a clean, sober young engineer after a bad experience with the previous second. As in my engine room debut on the first tanker, the well-trained crew assisted me, especially with maneuvering down the Mississippi.

The ship went to Norfolk, not my hoped-for destination of New York. I had planned to fly to Boston and see if distance really did make the heart grow fonder. But the chief was so pleased with my work that he refused to sign me off in Norfolk. Finally, after pleading and explaining my personal needs, I was relieved and caught the only flight to Boston. This proved to be my last seagoing trip as a merchant marine engineer. Ending by having my work appreciated was a confidence builder that later proved very helpful when I faced new challenges.

8

Another Turning Point

Time apart had helped the relationship between my woman friend and me to grow stronger and more meaningful. Wanting to be nearby and help with her three children, I rented a beachfront cottage from a Rockport friend. I continued to do some night engineering around the Boston area, along with occasional substitute teaching, but I was anxious to start my own seafood company. My previous schemes for revolutionizing the fishing industry were too grandiose; I was looking now for something on a smaller scale.

The father of Roy Moore, my Rockport friend, had been one of the pioneer lobster dealers in the area. After his death the small commercial wharf facility located in Pigeon Cove had been boarded up. Roy and I started off on a small scale as partners and renovated the old building and equipment. After a year we agreed that I should form a corporation and expand as sole owner.

Over the next thirty years and more, I ran the New England Lobster Company. For almost that same thirty years the relationship with my woman friend continued. As is true of most people, my business and personal lives experienced high points and low. The two were intertwined in so many ways that it is probably best for me just to let them flow together.

I started my lobster business with a capitalization of less than $1000 in a small building at the end of a wharf owned by a local drop-forge company. Two lobster holding tanks with about 2000 pounds capacity, a seawater circulating pump, a floor scale, and a pickup truck comprised my equipment to handle the daily catch of around ten lobstermen. I arranged with a large Boston lobster company to act as a kind of buying station. The company paid me 10 cents a pound over the going boat price. When I accumulated enough lobsters for a truckload, I would pack them in 100-pound crates and truck them to Boston in the early morning. I would usually be back in Pigeon Cove in time to receive the new catch and start the process all over again. When the lobstering was productive, I would make daily trips with around 1000 pounds, but usually it took a few days to accumulate a truck load.

Most of the old-time lobstermen started at daybreak and were finished by noon, so I had time to be with my friend. Her original home had been sold after her divorce and she was living in a small rental apartment with the three children. I helped her find a suitable three-bedroom house to buy in Pigeon Cove. We had lunch at various places and played a lot of cribbage to ease everyone's adjustment to the situation. Often I could arrange my schedule to be with her, but that became more difficult as the business grew. My friend's father had come to this country from Sweden as a young man and had become a successful businessman. He was very supportive of us and enjoyed coming down to the wharf and mingling with the old Scandinavian fishermen. He and I became fast friends and he was a helpful adviser to me.

ANOTHER TURNING POINT

As I took on more lobstermen for greater capacity and sales production, I had to expand the building that housed the company. I also established a local restaurant purveyor route and a retail fish market. Initially, temporary help was sufficient, but I soon needed a manager and full-time seasonal employees. With the assistance of a manager, I was able to create more productive time for the relationship as well as other personal interests. Several successful real estate ventures enabled me to move from my rental cottage to a larger home and studio. I had developed an interest in sculpting, and I wanted space to pursue this new activity. During the off-season I was able to pursue my new interest in sculpting; I took private lessons and devoured every book I could locate on the subject. I was accepted into the New England Sculptors Association and later into the prestigious Rockport Art Association. I found working in stone, particularly marble, to be my favored medium. This artistic pursuit is part of my life to this day.

For some years my company was fairly successful despite strong competition. I established a fish market at the entrance to historic Bearskin Neck in Rockport and operated a seafood restaurant in the Folly Cove section of Cape Ann. I also partnered with Essex friends in a 20-acre marina. It was satisfying to own potentially valuable property in that I was in a vulnerable rental situation on the wharf.

Eventually I broke away from the Boston connection and started doing my own grading, packing, and shipping to the Fulton Fish Market in New York City. With growing financial success I felt confident enough to discuss marriage with my friend. We both knew the complications of children aged thirteen, twelve, and seven, to say nothing of my trying to operate a small competitive business. Still, our emotions ran very deep. It was her father who stepped in to point out the reality of our situation; he believed that such a family obligation would destroy me. We eventually followed his advice and for years maintained a beautiful European-style relationship. Her marriage to another man who could provide greater stability for her children and her many medical setbacks did not impede our relationship. When the two girls were old enough, I helped establish new lives for them in my adopted winter vacation state of Arizona. Her son graduated from college, went his own way and remained in Rockport. After our time of sharing a life that few people would understand, my friend died, and a few years later, my business came to a close – events that opened up a new chapter in my life.

9

The Hawaiian Islands

During my New England Lobster Company years, I made two visits to Hawaii in the early 1970s. The first involved escorting my mother on her first air flight. She was going to visit my brother in Auckland, New Zealand. At the time, John was a microscope research photographer. The doctor he worked with at Massachusetts General Hospital had received a research grant to New Zealand and John was included. While there he renewed a relationship with an Australian girl with whom he had corresponded since his navy days. They married and started a family.

My mother was afraid she would never see her two granddaughters, so I agreed to fly as far as Honolulu and accompany her during a restful stopover of a few days. News of the time of our arrival must have traveled fast from back home in Gloucester, for we received a lei greeting at the airport from a lovely young graduate of the University of Hawaii. Penny was the sister of one of my high school classmates and was now a cub crime reporter for the *Honolulu Star Bulletin*. It must have been a difficult assignment for such a petite girl, but she came from a tough, competitive seafaring family. The famous waterfront sculpture in Gloucester, Man at the Wheel, was modeled after her grandfather, Captain Clayton Morrissey.

OAHU

Penny was a calming influence on my mother and made my escort job easier. She drove us to our hotel overlooking Waikiki Beach and arranged to meet us the next day for an island tour. The tour which took us completely around the island of Oahu was a culture shock. I remember Diamond Head, the Pali tunnel, Makapuu Bay, watching surfers on the North Shore, and even wading in to feel the powerful pull of the Pacific Ocean. We drove down through sugarcane fields to Pearl Harbor and back to Waikiki. Her knowledge of the island was phenomenal; she pointed out sights and explained in a manner the regular tourist would probably never experience. Her presentation and obvious love for the islands persuaded me to stay another week and visit more of Hawaii than just Oahu.

The next day I took my mother to the airport. Despite a long, nervous wait for the Air New Zealand flight to Auckland, the multiethnic "people-watching" proved to be a great escape. The thing that really eased my mother's anxiety was the arrival of a Tongan family in festive native dress. They were seeing their grandfather off. He apparently was some kind of chief, for they sang and danced in true ceremonial fashion. It was one of many magic moments that I was to experience. My mother had a fulfilling visit in New Zealand and gained enough confidence to return without my assistance.

With Mother on her way, I proceeded to turn native for a week. Returning to Pearl Harbor was a needed first stop, followed by a little cultural education at the Bishop Museum. I also went back to the Makapuu Oceanic Center and introduced myself to Tap Pryor as owner of the New England Lobster Company. I had read of his involvement in aquaculture. Tap was the son of one of the Pan American Airline pioneers. As a child, he had sat at the feet of Charles Lindbergh and other visionaries as they described planes that would carry passengers. He was trying to be a pioneer himself in the field of aquaculture.

Our mutual interests almost led to my teaming up with Tap for a lobster-raising farm in the sugarcane fields on Molokai. I have not been in touch with Tap for over thirty years, but am glad to hear he is still fighting for the right to harvest the sea. In my mind, aquaculture is the best approach to the future.

(I once had a confrontation with the Reverend Sun Myung Moon, when he came into Gloucester with his deep pockets and faithful following. My advice to him was to concentrate on farming the sea instead of developing unfair commercial exploitation. It must have had some impact on him, for one Christmas I received a gift of very special ginseng tea from the reverend, and "Moonie" pressure on the waterfront eased.)

I was starting to get almost a spiritual feeling that I had been to Hawaii before. While visiting the state capitol I was drawn to a large-than-life bronze statue of Father Damien, founder of the leper colony on Molokai. Strange things started to happen. The following accounts may be vague or disjointed, but this is how they remain in my memory.

MAUI

In the 1970s, Hawaiian Airlines offered deals to fly to the various islands for one low fare, and I think a car rental deal was thrown in. My first trip was to Maui. I had a rental car but no place to stay the night I arrived. The places of my choosing were already filled, so I stayed at a youth hostel. The tip-off was the hundred bicycles out front. It was like a military barrack room and had shared beds. After my time at MMA, homophobia did not exist for me; still, when I had to crawl into bed with a youth from who-knew-where, I almost told the manager, "I'll sleep in the rental car." But it was very late and I was exhausted. As it was, the kid beside me was just as frightened, so we curled up in opposing fetal positions and slept the night away. Next morning I treated him and a few of his world-traveling friends to breakfast. They could not understand why an American with a car would stay at such a place. Little did they know me or some of the other adventures that would follow on Maui!

There is no need to go into the beauty of this island; I'll just say it was spectacular. My first stop was the old whaling town of Lahaina, probably because of the Gloucester and New Bedford influence. I could say I had a "whale of a time", but I'll spare you further description.

Next was driving up to Haleakala Crater. Traveling through clouds was a strange experience for the car and for me. I had been warned of the need for high-altitude gas adjustment, but as usual I ignored the advice. Somehow it was corrected and we got to the top. There I was called by some power to go down into the crater. Talk about moon walking!! The stillness in the air and feeling of total isolation made me want to break into an "Om Mane Padre Om" Buddhist mantra.

The silence was soon broken by a figure emerging from the lunar landscape. He appeared to be one of the '60s hippies still hanging about. My question was serious, "What the hell are you doing living in here?" His answer: "I chose this place to live because the world will experience major destruction. There will be earthquakes and floods. The earth will be covered by water. Haleakala is shaped like a saucer. I will float about inside this saucer until a new world is formed. Do you want to stay and be part of this new world?" Needless to say, my exit up the steep slope was rapid.

My next venture in the rental car was down the spectacular but dangerous Hana highway - dangerous because there is eye-diverting beauty at every turn. Beyond the native recommendation, "You should drive down to Hana", I had other interests. I recalled from a Tap Pryor conversation that Charles Lindbergh's resting place was in Hana, and this drew me more than that local tourist advice. On the way down I picked up a couple of guys and their hippie princesses. They were on the way to meditate and dive through lava tubes to Lindbergh's burial site. My memory may play tricks on me, but I think this is what really happened...

After going through Hana, we approached an area that seemed innocuous. Scrambling up a jungle-like embankment, we came upon several placid pools. The so-called flower children dove in and never surfaced. Curiosity led me into one of the boldest experiences of my life. I dove in too. The first shallow pool had only one outlet, so I went down through a lava tube and came up in another beautiful pool. Lush foliage was everywhere and the Pacific Ocean was visible in the distance. A dive into another subterranean lava tube led to another pool. This continued until I was near the ocean's edge. I finally met the others and we went on foot to Lindbergh's resting place. It seemed like a strange final setting for a man who had been so involved in controversial historical events.

MANY LANDS MANY HEARTS

MOLOKAI

The trip from Maui to Molokai was a real puddle jump. Again I rented a car and this time found a nice beachfront motel unit, I think near Kaunakakai. I could look across the channel and see Maui. By this time I was getting into the island spirit. One morning when beachcombing for shells, I came upon a native teacher showing a group of young students the old way of catching fish. He would get up on a high point in order to see the schools of fish. Once he sighted them, he would throw a net out in a circular motion hoping to surround the fish. The students would wade out in the surf and slowly purse the net and tow it to shore. It was great to see someone teaching the old ways.

After observing several net tosses, I was invited to participate. Now I was really going native! This crude beaching of the shiny, slithery fish was such a contrast to the sophisticated methods used back home in Gloucester. The teacher told me he sang with a group at a local nightspot. They only sang the old traditional chants, not the Don Ho variety, and asked if I would like to attend. I guess he sensed I was not your typical "haole" (mainland visitor). I was delighted and that night after listening to several songs, the spotlight went to my table and I was given the opportunity to choose a song. Well, the only song I could think of that would capture this wonderful day was, "I am going to a hukelau", the fishing song. There was a little gasp from the singers, but they politely honored my request. To this day, it's one of the things I wish I could take back. Why I didn't, in my stupidity, ask them to sing one of their favorite island songs, I'll never know. I did manage to save grace upon leaving by acknowledging my touristy mistake.

The next day I spent going up to the cliffs overlooking the leper colony. Apparently my fascination with the Father Damien statue had lured me, for now I was looking down from the Ka-laupapa Pali to the colony below. After a strange mesmerizing moment, I saw some natives going down the trail on mules carrying supplies and mailbags. The lure was too strong for me, so I got in line and followed behind. Three miles and twenty-six switchbacks later, I was standing in the leper colony.

I had read that the affliction known as Hanson's disease was not contagious, and my strange arrival was met with smiles and waves. The little community was complete, even to a town hall that housed local sculpture — and even to a local sheriff. He approached me and yelled, "How the hell did you get here?" His arm tried to hide his contorted, tooth-decayed mouth. "Down the trail, sir", I answered. "Well, up the trail you'll return." He escorted me to the base and made sure I departed. (Years later, watching a PBS special on the colony, I saw my sheriff friend again. He was being interviewed and turned out to be originally from Vermont. He still used mouth covering gestures, but they resulted from vanity and had nothing to do with leprosy.) The trip back was exhausting, but every upward step brought an inner joy of accomplishment. I had fulfilled some unanswered calling.

HAWAII

My time was running out, but I wanted to at least visit the Big Island. I flew into Kona Airport and found another rental car despite the ongoing gasoline shortage. Newspapers had horror stories of long waiting lines and major transportation disruptions on the mainland. I was lucky to be away. Hawaii is the largest island of the chain and in a whirlwind two days I managed to hit all the highlights. I stayed that first night overlooking Kona Bay and witnessed the most dramatic sunset I have ever seen. The next day I explored the Kona area and drove to Kilauea Volcano Park. On the way I viewed house lots for sale right in old lava flows. I must confess, I took some lava as a souvenir not knowing that the lava was thought to be the tears of Madam Pele, the fire goddess, and that bad luck would come to those who made off with it. I became aware of this curse, after experiencing a string of misfortunes; I returned the lava to one of our Hawaiian seafood buyers in a box of lobsters he had ordered. To my amazement, life ever since has been far more joyous and fulfilling.

After a quick tour around the seaport of Hilo, I hiked into an area known for its pristine beauty and waterfalls, and then up to the Royal Macadamia Farm. It was a fairly new venture and seemed to offer opportunity for investment, but I never followed through. Every time I munch on these delicious nuts, it brings back pleasant memories.

As I recall, the trip back to Kona Airport was along a highway flanked by the ocean on one side and cattle farms sloping up to the mountains of Mauna Loa and Mauna Kea on the other. Laurence Rockefeller was developing an exclusive golf and beach resort along the coast. The plane back to Honolulu meant an end to my island hopping. I departed for Boston with deep spiritual feelings for these islands, and I knew I would return.

KAUAI

Beautiful Kauai. I was told if you cannot pronounce the name, call it "cow eye". After visiting Oahu, Maui, Molokai, and the Big Island in one whirlwind tour in 1973, my time ran out and I missed Kauai. I think it was two years later that I arranged to visit my brother in New Zealand. At the time, an incredible travel deal was available for around $1000 allowing unlimited major stops around the world within a one-year time period. I had only two months to play with, but every moment was well spent.

I'll begin with the return to Hawaii and finally seeing Kauai. I arrived in Lihue, rented a car, and headed for the north side of the island. My first goal was to hike the trails on the Na Pali coast. I joined up with a young woman from Harrisburg, Pennsylvania, who was hiking alone. Diehard hippies were camped out throughout the islands, still trying to find themselves and experiment in all possible ways. This hiking companion was into fruits and nuts, and I guess I fit the latter category. She was a helpful guide along the trail, for she knew some of the people we encountered. The trails wound 4000 feet along the coast and down into many lush valleys. Plenty of fruit and water were available, so one could stay there indefinitely, but I had checked into a Hanalei motel and only planned a day hike.

The following day I skipped the Fern Grotto, as it looked too commercial, and went instead to Waimea Canyon. It is considered the Grand Canyon of the South Pacific, and I must say it was spectacular. I observed other sites, including ponds and work by the Menehune, the spiritual little people, before departing for Honolulu and my flight across the Pacific.

10

The Pacific and the Far East

Returning to Honolulu after finally touring Kauai, I was ready to continue on and visit my brother in New Zealand. The first stop was Pago Pago (pronounced Pango Pango for some strange reason) in American Samoa. Since I was in the lobster business, I checked out the local fishery, but found it to be a primitive diving activity. This being American-controlled Samoa, I also visited the U.S. Department of Fisheries and toured the major tuna factories. Van Camp and other companies had their strongholds here.

The trip over to Western Samoa, a separate island and not part of the United States, was far more interesting. I stayed in Apia at the world-famous Aggie Grey's. It was a collection of rambling bungalows set in lush gardens. The wooden louvered windows opened out to walkways of hanging bananas and the flowers that were everywhere.

Aggie was an old lady when I met her, but still as gracious as when she had entertained our troops during WWII. She had powerful connections and always had hamburgers, cokes, and ice cream for "the boys". James Michener started writing his *Tales of the South Pacific* at her resort. Robert Louis Stevenson spent his last years here, and I had a chance to visit his gravesite. The common dining room once served all the important politicians, Hollywood stars, and traveling royalty. Gary Cooper, Marlon Brando, William Holden, and many more had been there. Somerset Maugham's play *Rain* and the ensuing movie versions of *Sadie Thompson* were inspired by this woman and this setting. It was later torn down but replaced almost intact, with her son carrying on the hospitable tradition.

I left Samoa for Fiji feeling a part of the human experience. I carried with me the laughter of war-weary soldiers and a deep sense of being close to literary giants. Oceania has a strange pull on the senses!!!

FIJI

My arrival in Suva, Fiji was greeted by the highest heat and humidity I think I have ever encountered. The original plan was to stay at the Grand Pacific Hotel. This used to be the choice British place to stay with its high teas and other traditional splendor, but it was going downhill. An age was passing to newer modern beachfront resorts. I shared a taxi from the airport with a couple of young worldly backpackers. They forewarned me about the Grand Pacific and recommended a small hotel that was on their insider list of places to stay. I took note, but still followed my itinerary.

The hotel was huge. It looked like you could fit a soccer field in the lobby. The floors were tiled and there appeared to be more potted ferns then people. I was greeted by a big barefooted Fijian wearing a white shirt and sula. This wraparound sarong skirt (also known as lava lava) seemed rather unmasculine, but was certainly practical for the weather there.

After I checked in, he took my bags and led me down a long dimly lit corridor to my room. The absence of other guests made me wonder why I was being placed in a wing so far from the main lobby. The door opened to a dark room, probably to keep out the heat and conserve energy. The absence of life changed as soon as he turned on the light. The room came alive with the largest cockroaches I have ever seen. They were all over the tiled floor, up the walls, on the ceiling. I yelled, "No way am I staying here." The porter nonchalantly said "No problem", and started to stomp the roaches with his bare feet.

I took my bags, checked out, and walked the downtown streets until I came to the little hotel that my backpacker friends had mentioned. The humidity and heat were terrible. I forget the name of this place, and I am sure it no longer exists, but it was on a hill and owned by an Australian lawn bowls champion. He checked me in with a chuckle after I told of my experience at the Grand Pacific. When he learned I was going to visit my brother in Auckland, he lit up and invited me to the third-floor rooftop lounge. It was the only place around that caught a semblance of a breeze. The owner had several friends in Auckland who owned small hotel taverns, and before I departed he gave me a letter of introduction. On the back of an oversized business card made of sliced woven bamboo he wrote: *"Introducing my American friend, Charles L. Fields. He is all wool and a yard wide."* Later this card provided many drinks and meals in New Zealand; I could not pay for anything. I guess lawn bowling champions pull a lot of weight down under?

The following day I saw huge headlines in the Suvan paper: *Charles Arrives*. This came as a complete surprise to me; I thought I was quietly making my way across the Pacific. Upon further reading I discovered it was Prince Charles who had arrived. He really got into the native thing wearing a custom-made sula and attempting to direct downtown traffic. What a fool he made of himself!

My experiences around Suva included snorkeling, a sport I never mastered; drinking yagona from a kava bowl, a local custom I never wanted to master; and being overwhelmed by the invasion of East Indians. They seemed to control all the shops and were making inroads into controlling the politics as well. Now, after a military coup, the government is back in Fijian hands. Not too far removed from cannibalism, the Fijians are a fierce, proud people. Despite the missionary influence, I knew I should respect their customs. Never wear a hat in their villages or homes. Never touch a child's head with an affectionate pat or you could end up in the stewpot as had many a missionary.

My departure for New Zealand was from Nadi. The bus ride from Suva went along the developing beach resort areas. Fiji was coming into the new era of era of jet travel. Maybe out of the pot into another fire? It was one of the few places left with pristine beauty and innocence.

NEW ZEALAND

As I start this description of my trip to the North Island of New Zealand, can you read, pronounce, and tell the meaning of this word? Hint: It is the longest place name in the world. Taumatawhakatangihangakoauauotamateaturipukakakapimaungahronukupokaiwhenuakitanatahu. (Translation: The brow of the hill where Taumata, the man with the big knees slid, climbed, and swallowed the mountains, to travel the land and play his flute to his beloved one.) The name is usually shortened to Taumata if that is any help.

Auckland in the 1970s was just starting to experience urban renewal. My brother, being a serious professional photographer, captured all the old Victorian buildings and important architectural features of downtown. He had witnessed urban renewal and loss of the pictorial history back in the States and wanted to make sure this did not happen in New Zealand. Years later his book, *Victorian Auckland,* became the definitive source of how things used to look. In New Zealand it spurred the comment, "It took a Yank to show us."

I spent several weeks traveling about Auckland and was particularly impressed with the pubs and wonderful beer. The only problem was the 6:00pm closing time. I had never seen so much beer swigged down in such a short time. People literally reeled out of the pubs and into the streets at this early closing hour and commuted home. I understand that this foolish law has since been eliminated.

After exploring most of the North Island, I booked a ten-day package plan to the South Island. The trip began with a flight to Queenstown. Flying over Wellington, the capital, I could see the division of the two islands and sensed that the two were vastly different. Queenstown is a four-season alpine town on Lake Wakatipu. I stayed at a very proper inn. It was my first experience with formal British table settings. There were all kinds of forks to the left and knives and spoons to the right. I remembered from my mess-cook days on the training ship, "Always work from the outside in." The thing was there we had only two utensils - if we were lucky. The real problem now was what to do with all the utensils lying parallel above my plate. Common sense and social survival skills learned at MMA came to the fore once again: "Observe and follow those around you." But they were eating with the fork in the left hand and cutting with the knife in the right. This made sense, but it was totally disruptive to my hand-changing upbringing.

The following day I crossed the lake to an island sheep station. Sheep were everywhere, but the real attraction was the dogs. Watching them perform their herding duties made me want to recruit them as wide receivers for a professional football team. When checking the correct spelling for the lake in later years, I learned that the island sheep station is now a golf course. I am almost sorry I did this research.

My next planned trip was a flight into Milford Sound but it was canceled by fog, so I spent an extra day flying up to explore the Mount Cook glacier. Quite exciting landing on a glacier! After all it was Sir Edmund Hillary's mountain training territory. He later climbed Mount Everest "because it was there". Now it was part of a tourist package.

Next day it was on to Christchurch by train. Observing the mix of people traveling was an experience in itself: the usual business types, family groups, and tourists from all over. The Japanese and Germans seemed to dominate. My compartment section was filled with a group of wild pig hunters. They had been in the bush for two weeks and their tales of hits and misses grew with each passing pint. Christchurch itself is neatly laid out. I personally found it too flat and too perfectly landscaped, but the people were wonderful.

I flew back to Auckland and after a few final days left John and his family. It was a tearful goodbye, for I didn't know if I would ever see them again. This trip had been one of those once in-a-lifetimes.

HONG KONG

To my regret, I never got to Australia. The plane flew over Sydney and Queensland, then crossed over New Guinea and the Philippines. As I looked down on this area, I couldn't help thinking of WWII. The pilot pointed out sunken wreckage, and the clear blue water seemed to magnify the images. But from 30,000 feet the sea and the islands looked calm and "in place".

Our arrival in Kowloon, China was similar to the air acrobatics on Mount Cook, for the wings seemed to touch the rooftops. Years later the new Hong Kong International Airport, an engineering wonder, eliminated this disaster waiting to happen.

A taxi brought me to the Ambassador Hotel. It had been recommended by the Chinese owners of the hotel where I had stayed in Honolulu. It seemed their cousin owned the Ambassador. Strange things take over when traveling. I remember the saying, "You don't take a trip, let the trip take you."

The Ambassador was within walking distance of the ferry to Hong Kong and in the middle of all the business and entertainment activities. My first impression of China was SO MANY PEOPLE! The sights, smells, and sounds made my senses come alive. It was almost too much of a change from the rustic life of New Zealand.

My room was adequate but after all the lights were out and the hotel was quiet, I could hear rats scurrying through the walls and ceiling. They sounded big and I was afraid they would chew through. Frightening as it seemed in crowded, overbuilt China,

I figured this was a common occurrence. After an unsettled sleep, I walked down to the Star ferry to cross over to Hong Kong.

The ferry was filled with merchants, tourists and humanity of all description. Hong Kong loomed as Manhattan does when approached from Staten Island, but the tall buildings appeared even more impressive. At the terminal, I was greeted by a powerful Henry Moore sculpture. This oversized bronze, with its abstract amorphous form, was perfectly placed. Hong Kong rose behind it waiting for my invasion.

If I thought the throngs of people in Kowloon were huge, they were nothing compared to this moving mass. It was almost too much of a cultural shock. I found a peaceful escape by taking the tram up to Victoria Peak. There I could get my bearings. Off to the west was Happy Valley, the racetrack and sporting area. To the east I saw the Aberdeen fish docks, and out in the harbor, surrounded by commercial ships and colorful junks, was the jumbo ornate floating restaurant called Tai Pak. I had noticed the marketplace when going to the tram and thought it would be interesting to explore some evening.

I planned my tentative itinerary while up on the peak. That first day I decided to make a slow adjustment to the masses of people by taking a bus to the Happy Valley racetrack. The horses ran in the opposite direction to our tracks and the betting was very confusing, but I had a fun day. It was equally confusing and fun to watch cricket matches on the carefully manicured lawns nearby. I never did find out what "sticky wicket" meant...

One other memory was the Chinese fascination with my Dexter hiking boots. I was offered many new custom suits if I would sell my boots. Perhaps they wanted to copy them for future cheap exports. Perhaps they thought I had a hidden spy compartment. Who knows?

The Star ferry back to Kowloon at commuter time was like rush hour traffic in any city in the world. I was glad to get back to the hotel, where it was cool and peaceful. I guess the rats were resting up for their nightly forays.

That night I had a foolish shrimp feast. Foolish because I wanted to go a real Chinese restaurant, not a tourist spot. There were several nearby places, but to be sure of authenticity I followed a Chinese group into a small family restaurant. After I was seated, all eyes were watching my next move. I wanted shrimp and pointed to a plate on a nearby table. The waiter showed me the character for shrimp on the menu which did not have the usual numbered choices. I pointed to several shrimp selections. The waiter seemed a little startled, but took the order. Next thing I knew a huge tray of shrimp dishes came to my table - in every imaginable combination. I was too stubborn to admit my ordering mistake, so I tried to eat through this seafood banquet. You could sense the amazement of the families. Children stared and I think the Chinese men, being gamblers, were taking bets on my ability to eat through it all. I saved face by doing it justice, but made sure I had advice in English from then on.

Before retiring to my room or maybe to avoid the nocturnal rodent ruckus, I ventured to the Ambassador's cocktail lounge. It was fairly late and I was sitting alone. A well-dressed middle-aged woman came to my table. Poised and educated, she was obviously a "working woman". Her questioning led to why I was alone. "Are you looking for a man?" My answer must have satisfied her, for she quickly joined me for a drink. What followed was educational and satisfying in every way.

She claimed she had been a successful prostitute when younger and had invested her money in apartment houses. In fact, she boasted of being one of the largest property owners in Kowloon. Her English was clipped and perfect. Apparently she continued to cruise the bars to fulfill her needs, or maybe just to test her abilities to still attract men. I must say she was no longer beautiful, but her seductive ways were intact.

In the morning she promised to return at noon to give me a personal tour and a special lunch at the world-famous Peninsula Hotel. I told her my funds were dwindling, that I had just enough to complete the trip home. No problem, I was to be her guest. We toured her vast apartment holdings and at the Peninsula she was greeted like royalty.

The lunch there under her direction was dim sum. This was all new to me. Waiters brought little covered bowls of all kind of delicacies on a cart. After you made your selections and ate, the empty bowls were totaled at the end of the meal for the bill. Good food, good company, proper portions, and I was even told in English what I was eating. However, I was beginning to have the distinct feeling that something was amiss. We returned to the hotel and I told my companion that I wasn't feeling well. I said, "Maybe a shrimp reaction." We arranged to tour Hong Kong the next day, but when she knocked at my door in the morning I ignored it.

Hours later I took the ferry to Hong Kong and checked out the fishing industry, dined on the floating Tai Pak, browsed the marketplace, and boldly ventured by train to the recently opened New Territories. It was all a great educational experience, but the masses of people were too overwhelming.

THE PACIFIC AND THE FAR EAST

BANGKOK

Bangkok is an old city, one that always will be old despite the modern wheeling and dealing. Perhaps I should start with the mysterious disappearance of the Thai silk king Jim Thompson.

He was an OSS agent who remained in Bangkok after World War II and cornered the Thai silk industry. Even after I arrived the locals were still wondering what had happened to Jim. He simply disappeared in 1967. No trace. His wealthy sister was later found bludgeoned to death in Philadelphia. His Thai home is now a museum.

I stayed at the Oriental Hotel in Bangkok. Thompson, an avid art and antique collector, had been trying to bring it back to its grander days. The hotel, Like Aggie Grey's in Samoa, was another haunt of Somerset Maugham's (Our paths seemed to be always crossing, let's hope some of his writing genius rubbed off.) Construction was at a standstill during my visit, but I heard later that the Oriental went on to become a world-class hotel.

The first morning there stands out in my mind. I was having coffee and reading the paper in the lobby. Suddenly I looked up to see a well-dressed Thai leading a baby elephant up to the front desk. He discussed some business, then he and the elephant casually walked out. I was the only curious person. Welcome to Bangkok.

A slow stroll on the wide sidewalks and in the garden areas was a nice way to be introduced to the city. Every park had elaborate kites flying overhead in mock battle. I was told some people placed pieces of sharp glass in their kite tails to slice down an opponent.

In order to view more of the city I hired a taxi. One cab ride wiped out all my earlier pleasant experiences. The noise… the traffic… the exhaust pollution… and bumper maniacs forced me to seek a more peaceful plan for day two.

I had been told by friends from Montreal who took a world tour by ship, not to miss the Klong boat trip. Bangkok is called the Venice of the East because of its river life. Families and businesses live and trade on the river; houseboats are everywhere. A guided tour brings visitors alongside and into the lives of these boat people. (It is also possible to tour the islands of the sacred golden temples.) The motorized Klong boat carried us into the teak forest. We witnessed elephants hauling huge teak logs to a saw mill. The animals were prodded and gouged, but animal rights activists were nowhere to be seen. The stock answer was, "They are like your draft horses, just doing a job." The last event on our tour was a Thai luncheon, an exhibition of ancient dance and music with a finale of exuberant Thai boxers getting a kick out of one another.

My last day before flying to Athens was spent at one of Jim Thompson's stores buying yards of Thai silk. My funds were getting perilously low, but I knew I would be hexed by every female acquaintance if I did not return with some of this magic weave. The poor little worms eating mulberry leaves throughout their lives, only to be boiled for strands of raw silk! One cocoon could yield 700 yards of filament. The dying, drying, and hand-weaving were long processes, but so exquisitely rewarding.

PACIFIC AND BACK

The whirlwind tours of Hong Kong and Bangkok must have left me a bit addled. I am not certain, but I think I spent some time at the Taj Mahal. I know I changed planes in New Delhi from Cathay Pacific to Nigerian Airlines. I either had been there in a past life, which is possible, or I had time for a bus tour from New Delhi. I know that every time I see pictures of the Taj Mahal I have a flood of memories. One in particular: I had to use the men's room, which was as large as a marbled museum. The gent next to me was having difficulty because his right hand was handcuffed to an Evergreen Air attaché case. I discreetly acknowledged his predicament and walked away. Evergreen Air was a CIA cover during and after the Vietnam War. Certainly I didn't want to be accused of assisting the CIA in India.

Speaking of airplanes, I flew many different lines and Cathay Pacific impressed me. I was a little leery of boarding the Nigerian plane, but the service and ethnic food were wonderful, especially the fresh fruit and dark brewed "real" coffee. The stewards were dressed in fashionable native style and had a genuine concern for the passengers. The trip to Athens was at night, but I did manage to see the snow-capped Himalayas. An old friend who had lived and studied in India during the time of the Raj once told me, "In Sanskrit, it is pronounced *Him mal yas,* not *Him a lay as,* and it means, "Abode of the Snow".

At last I arrived in Athens and took a bus to a small inexpensive hotel in the seaport of Piraeus. The owner, naturally, had many relatives in the Boston area. The hotel was within walking distance of the central harbor. The inner basin was filled with fishing boats mixed in with small and large luxury yachts. The outer harbor and docks were busy with commercial vessels from all over the world. Piraeus is where you get fine fresh seafood, and I vowed not to repeat my gluttonous shrimp mistake. In the restaurant I chose, you pointed out what you wanted from a live fish tank. My selection was perfectly prepared.

MANY LANDS MANY HEARTS

The next day I took the bus to Athens. Walking about the city, I observed the democratic way; it seemed that every street corner had an orator speaking out on his principles. I took the typical tourist trip to the Acropolis, and standing in the marble ruins chilled me to the core. Had I been here as well in a past life?

I almost couldn't leave Athens. As I mentioned, my financial situation was dire. While walking around the city, I had noticed many young travelers hanging about outside the American Express office. Their funds were tapped out too and they were waiting for money from home. My American Express card was used up, but I had enough for cab fare to the airport the next morning. The taxi arrived at the little hotel courtyard at 5:00am. As I was checking out, the proprietor noticed the care with which I was counting my money and he asked, "Do you have enough for the cab and the $15 airport debarkation fee?" I had not expected this extra expense and explained my predicament. He tried negotiating with the cabbie. Hands were flying and there was much shaking of the cab driver's head. The dynamic Greek exchanges caused windows to open with more shouting. I think they were all yelling, "It's 5am! Shut up!!" The proprietor said, "He wants his regular fare, so I'll take care of it. But if you meet any of my relatives back in Boston, give them a few lobsters." With the deal done and many *efharistos* (thanks), I escaped Greece on Ari's Olympic Airlines for London.

The eight-hour wait in London's Heathrow Airport for my flight to Boston seemed like an eternity. I had no money left for anything, not even a cup of coffee. Talk about playing it close! At least I enjoy people watching and airports are definitely the best places for that. Finally I boarded and was seated for the last leg of my around-the-world journey. Luck must have been with me throughout this trip, for I had survived some unusual situations.

It seemed to still be with me, for my seatmate turned out to be Dr. Vaughn Anthony of the National Marine Fisheries, returning from a conference in Oslo. At the time, I was on the Massachusetts State Marine Fisheries Commission. Dr. Anthony and I had met in the past on many fishery-related problems, but never on a personal level. When the beverage cart appeared, I quickly, without any embarrassment, explained my financial plight. He understood and proved to be very generous. After several scotch whiskies over the Atlantic, the world's fishery problems were solved and a strong personal relationship was established. A fine ending to a fine trip!

11

Changes Professional and Personal

The experience of world travel helped prepare me for the changes that would occur in my business and personal life. By this time my daughter had moved with her mother to Florida and during my prearranged visits I would try to locate a potential vacation property. The only part of Florida that interested me was the Sarasota area. I had friends living there, as well as in Boca Raton, but neither coast really appealed to me. I gave up trying to find a seasonal escape in Florida and followed up on a vow to return to the southwest. I had visited Tucson in the late '60s to assist with the rental car driving of two older friends. I squired them everywhere; even though it was only a week's visit, the images stayed with me. Ten years later I returned and purchased a condo in Fountain Hills.

During a winter vacation in my new condo I received a call from my company manager. He said, "Come home, everything is gone." I knew a fierce blizzard had been expected in the area, but I never envisioned its severity or the damage it would cause. The sea had crashed over the breakwater, engulfed my lobster building, which was over 30 feet high, and washed everything into the harbor.

With the assistance of the Small Business Administration I built a bigger and better facility. Looking back, I probably should have heeded the fates. The increased expense of the improved facility meant more aggressive selling to the New York market. Two of our major accounts fell on hard times and went into bankruptcy; we were stuck with almost half a million dollars in useless accounts receivable. Despite using extreme structural precautions during the rebuilding, another fluke storm came and again caused severe damage. The need for more SBA lending created a severe burden.

My misfortunes were complicated by the closing of the Cape Ann Tool Company. Competition from foreign steel and the business climate in general led to its being put up for sale. The problem I faced was that the tool company owned the entire wharf and leased it to the town. I, in turn, leased from the town at a reasonable rate and thought the situation fairly safe. Everything seemed all right until the owners of the factory received offers from buyers who wanted to raze the plant and build a hotel-marina complex. I was caught in a land-usage dilemma.

The fishermen became very concerned by these proposals, for they feared they might lose access to the wharf and their moorings. They formed a fishermen's cooperative that negotiated a lease/purchase plan with the town and gradually squeezed me out of business. After several years of trying to operate under very restrictive conditions, I had no choice but to declare bankruptcy. The fishermen eventually got control of the wharf, including my building and equipment. To this day the tool company sits boarded up, facing development opposition from many environmental and regulatory groups. There was even a stage play written about the situation, *The Battle of Pigeon Cove Wharf*. My personal battle of stubbornly fighting the fates was over. I was free again.

I harbor, pardon the pun, no animosity toward the fishermen; they were acting to protect themselves. Despite my difficult times on the wharf, I have many fond memories, delivering over 300 cooked lobsters to the Coast Guard training ship *Eagle* when she was in port for the Tall Ships Event. Providing an "in the rough" lobster feed for the original Boston Patriots football team. A wild after-theater party with the cast of the touring musical, *The Fantastics*. I even had an impromptu afterhours lobster feed with John and Mime Bernard, a vacationing couple from Montreal. On their way to Cape Cod they stopped for breakfast at the Ralph Waldo Emerson Inn in Pigeon Cove. Looking down from the veranda, they saw the quaint wharf and stopped by to introduce themselves. They asked if I cooked lobsters and served the public. At the time I had a big outdoor lobster cooker for takeout only, but I agreed to meet them after closing for a personal feed. They arrived with wine and cheese and I cooked the lobsters. I had no dining area, so we simply sat on old shipping crates. That night was the beginning of a lifelong friendship. (They never did get to Cape Cod.) A few years later they introduced their daughter, the leading soap opera actress in Quebec Province to "Good Old Charlie". I think she was surprised to meet a young businessman and not a wizened fisherman. On a visit I made to Montreal, we were seen dining together and I became a mysterious *cause célèbre* in the local tabloids.

Also during those early business years, I met and formed an important friendship with Fred and Lucille Mulhauser from

Cambridge. Fred, after retiring as a partner with Superba Cravat, became director of the Salzburg Seminars in Austria. Through the Muhlhausers I met many impressive people. Among them were Peter Viereck, a Mount Holyoke professor and winner of the 1947 Pulitzer Prize for Poetry, and Harold Fleming, an eccentric writer of conservative corporate views. By coincidence, Harold corresponded with the author Ayn Rand. It was her book *The Fountainhead* that had been a strong influence on me and gave me entrepreneurial zeal.

John and Betty Schereschewsky, headmasters of Rumsey Hall in Washington, Connecticut, also come to mind. The private prep school was originally founded by Abercrombie and Fitch. Under the direction of the "Sherrys" it became a popular school and was associated with many literary and professional people, such as Arthur Miller and Marilyn Monroe and William and Rose Styron. Rose was the editor of the *Paris Review* and through Betty's influence I had my poetry, which I had been writing for many years, critiqued by Rose. The comments were very positive and encouraging.

Another dear friend who comes to mind is Charles Albert Hagner. Al was a Harvard graduate who studied in Munich during the Hitler movement. He befriended the composer Franz Kneisel and was introduced to the queen of Austria. He later studied metaphysical subjects and Sanskrit in India during the Raj uprising. He and I had a mutual liking for vodka that inspired many evenings of philosophical discourse.

Having lost my house during the bankruptcy in 1995, I rented a small riverfront house from John Hinckley, my trusted last employee. By coincidence, another former employee was trying to reestablish his family's chicken business. At one time he had been without work, and I found him employment at the lobster company and later at the marina. It now appeared that he could help me. The business he was trying to develop had a unique niche market that involved providing pedigree broiler chicks to a Chinese poultry company in New York City. When I teamed up with him my first thought was here I go again; dealing with perishables to New York - first bananas, then lobsters, and now chickens.

I started driving once a week a van filled with six thousand to eight thousand day-old chicks destined for raising farms in New York's Catskill Mountains area. I would usually leave before 4:00am. Circulation of natural cool air was critical to reduce the confined chick high body heat. I controlled the air flow by adjusting the windows. The raising farms were located in these mountains because of the mild conditions year-round.

The Catskills had once been a summer Mecca for New Yorkers. Irving Berlin was one of the first to lead the way for family vacationers. Large resorts followed with lavish facilities. The food and entertainment there became famous. Every major comedy or music act in the country probably had its start in the Catskills, also known as the Borscht Belt. Places such as Kutsher's and the Concord provided all conceivable amenities for a vacation. Grossinger's, "The Big G," in order to attract winter ski visitors was the first in the world to use artificial snow.

The decline of the Catskills resort industry began in the 1960s because city dwellers were moving into air-conditioned homes in the suburbs, and air travel to more exotic places became affordable. The resorts tried everything, but could not attract new young guests. Even the famous Woodstock event didn't help. During the time I was delivering, the area was considered to be in an economic blight. I witnessed the Grossinger's foreclosure and the demolition of the Concord.

As expected, land was cheap. My Chinatown connection was acquiring property and contracting out to local farmers to raise special broiler birds for the high-end Chinese restaurant market. The family business I was working for was one of the oldest in the country that dealt with special breeding. Through experimentation, a line of birds was created that economically offered just the right color and fat content for this market. I found this new business fascinating and eventually moved from part-time driver to hatchery manager.

I used to visit and explore other sites in the area after unloading the chicks. One memorable place was Zane Grey's home on the banks of the Upper Delaware River. I learned that before becoming the Father of the Western Novel, he had been a professional baseball player, a dentist, and a record-holding fisherman. The homestead, now a museum, reflects all these interests. Earlier, on one of my Arizona side trips, I had visited his wood cabin on the Mogollon Rim. Unfortunately the cabin and all the memorabilia in it were destroyed in a massive forest fire.

I paid other enjoyable visits on my way back home. The Baseball Hall of Fame at Cooperstown, New York, and Tanglewood, the summer home of the Boston Symphony Orchestra in the Berkshire town of Lenox, Massachusetts, come to mind. The visit to Cooperstown happened to be on the day a fantasy baseball game was scheduled. A group of older men pay to attend a baseball training camp and on the final day suit up and play a regulation game. The cheering section of wives, children, and in some cases grandchildren, was very rowdy. I watched with envy and fantasized about my own baseball days. The Tanglewood stop was also a special day, for Seiji Ozawa was conducting a rehearsal of Gershwin's *Rhapsody in Blue*. I sat in the acoustically designed shed with only a few other spectators and felt as if I were royalty.

The difficult declining years in the lobster business and now the new chicken venture had not allowed time for any personal creativity. In the past, I had been active with the New England Sculptors Association, and the Cambridge and Rockport Art Associations, exhibiting, jurying, and setting up shows. My sculpture had won many awards but I had become inactive. One night, when my brother was visiting from Australia, I received a call from a Rockport Art Association artist. The group was preparing a major exhibit of past and present sculptors and wanted me to enter a piece. My artistic side awakened, I entered one of my best marble sculptures. It was carved from Carrara marble. The stone had been a gift from Walker Hancock, one of the internationally famous sculptors being honored in the exhibit.

I had once met Walker and his wife on an American Airlines flight from Boston to Phoenix. He had been commissioned by Walter Annenberg to do his bust. The sitting was going to be at the Annenberg winter home in Palm Springs, but the Hancocks planned a week's stop in Phoenix. They had never been in the Valley of the Sun, so I offered to show them around. It was a great week of sharing thoughts and experiences. We did the museums, galleries, and Frank Lloyd Wright's Taliesin West.

It was during a Louise Nevelson exhibit at the Phoenix Art Museum that I had the opportunity to introduce Walker to my favorite Native American sculptor, Allan Houser. It was like east meeting west, for their work themes were totally different. I think this meeting resulted in Houser's recognition as not just an Indian artist but also as a sculptor of international quality. Houser was later was accepted into the prestigious National Sculpture

Society, owing in part, I am sure to Hancock's influence. I, in turn, received a block of Carrara marble for my Phoenix escort service. Many years passed before I had the courage to work the stone. I wanted it to be a worthy piece. It finally was completed and became one of my significant sculptures.

I should note here that Hancock helped save many of Europe's art treasures during World War II and gained wide attention for helping to complete the 69-foot Stone Mountain (Georgia) granite carving that memorialized confederate leaders Jefferson Davis, Robert E. Lee, and Stonewall Jackson. Hancock also created the 40-foot bronze Pennsylvania Railroad Memorial. His portrait busts included Presidents George H. Bush and Gerald Ford and poet Robert Frost to name a few. During the opening presentation of the Rockport Art Association sculpture exhibit, the ninety-year-old Walker Hancock was proudly escorted by President Bush's sister. It was a memorable event for me as well because this is where I met my wife-to-be.

Julia T. Marino was a fellow sculptor member of the RAA. I had admired her work, but we had never met. When I first saw this tall beautiful woman standing next to my sculpture, *Prayer Feather*, I thought she was the daughter of a longtime artist friend. After some stimulating opening conversation, she told me she had furniture disease. I asked, confused "What is that?" She replied, "It's when your chest falls into your drawers." The joke was cute, but totally unexpected. I realized she was not who I thought she was and I gasped, "Who *are* you?" She in turn said, "Who are *you*?" After awkward introductions, we viewed and admired each other's sculptures. I learned that Julia had been recently widowed and had a daughter with her own law practice. We spent the rest of the evening together mingling and finding complete joy in each other's company. A lunch date the next day started a relationship that we have lovingly shared ever since.

It seemed that my empty life was now full again. Julia and I had much in common and we realized through conversations about our past that fate had truly brought us together. The term "soul mate" is too often used, but here it fits perfectly. The days and weeks grew into months. That spring the two of us visited my daughter in Norfolk. She had graduated from Salem Teachers College and was married to a career navy man. They had two children.

After the family visit Julia and I continued on to explore Charleston and Savannah and then vacationed for a few days on beautiful Jekyll Island, South Carolina. On the coastal road north of Charleston, we stopped at the Brookgreen Sculpture Gardens. I had been there before on one of my Florida trips and had always wanted to share the experience with someone. The gardens had been converted from a rice plantation by Anna Hyatt Huntington, a wealthy, well-known sculptor, who had a summer studio in Gloucester. (Her commissioned bronze equestrienne statue of *Joan of Arc* stands in front of the American Legion building there.)

During that first visit I remembered being in awe of the sculptures that had been shipped in from all over the country and perfectly placed in the formal garden settings. I was especially impressed by Albin Polasek's *Man Carving His Own Destiny*, which depicted a heroic figure carving himself out of the stone. While in Florida, I had gone to Polasek's studio home in Winter Park. He had died, but his wife graciously gave me a complete tour. A reproduction of the Brookgreen sculpture stood at the entrance to the studio. According to his wife, he had completed the six-foot sculpture despite being assailed by a stroke. Amazingly, he had held and directed the chisel while an assistant struck the creative blows. Before leaving, I was given a signed copy of his book along with a warm personal message from his wife. Touring the Brookgreen Gardens now with someone who shared my love of the sculpture and surrounding landscape was worth the long wait. Before returning home we toured Jefferson's Monticello and completed the trip with a visit to Roosevelt's Hyde Park and the nearby Vanderbilt mansion.

The summer of 1998 Julia and I erected a small studio and outdoor carving tables at the back of her lovely home in Magnolia (a section of Gloucester), and I started doing some productive sculpting. I was a little concerned about the chipping noise, but the neighbors loved the sound of creativity. I became active again with the New England Sculptors Association and the Rockport Art Association.

After our second year together I decided it was time for us to visit Arizona. The sharing experience at Brookgreen Gardens had been very meaningful; I hoped that Julia would also enjoy the Southwest. Fortunately she loved the area and wanted to come back the next winter. Our return to Massachusetts in the spring found us actively sculpting, exhibiting and jurying shows.

One day while helping at the chicken farm, a feed supply augur clogged up I foolishly reached in to clean it, and one of my gloved fingers became caught. The machine was trying to pull in my hand and arm so I had to sacrifice one of my fingers to get free. I was alone with no means of communication. I compressed the bleeding and drove to the nearest medical facility. I ended up being driven by an ambulance to Brigham and Women's Hospital in Boston. My mother was in a nursing home at the time, and the only other person to contact was my soul mate, Julia. She drove into Boston with Adah Marker, a neighborhood friend, and I was released to her care. According to Julia, this is when she knew she truly loved me. Since our first meeting, the emotional transition had not been easy for her; after all, she had been married for over forty years. Her husband had been a retired naval officer who suffered the terrible effects of Agent Orange until his death. Apparently my love and my need were obvious enough to convince her of the true depth of this new relationship.

We decided it was best that my dog and I move into Julia's house during my recovery and therapy. Let me introduce Daisy, a strange combination of basset body and black Labrador head whom I inherited from my grandson. It was a kind gesture to replace my old dog, Rafer, who had been tragically run over while sleeping under a truck at the chicken farm.

After a few months of being on workmen's compensation, I received a modest settlement and decided finally to listen and follow the fates. I announced that I was retiring, making an end to the shipping of perishable goods such as bananas, lobsters, and chickens to New York City. I hoped it would be the beginning of shipping and exhibiting my sculpture there. Julia and I notified our daughters of our marriage plans and asked them to stand up for us in a simple oceanside ceremony at the Magnolia home. The friendship rings we had bought at the Hopi reservation during our winter visit to Arizona now became our wedding rings. It was a beautiful, quiet service.

The next day we traveled north to Vermont for a few days, stopping at the Carving Studio and other local marble supply sources. Lunch and a tour of the Von Trapp Family Lodge added a touch of music and romance. We returned to enjoyment of our retirement days and meeting with many well-wishers. At a pre-millennium marriage celebration more than a hundred friends shared our joy. After the Christmas and New Year holidays we prepared for a return trip to Arizona.

We repeated our marriage vows at the old Oraibi settlement at the Hopi reservation we had visited previously. And we wed once again in a more traditional setting, at the Chapel of the Holy Cross in Sedona. Both locales hold special significance for their cultures. I was pleased that the Southwest was becoming a part of both of us.

After a pleasant summer in Magnolia in the months following, we signed up for a local charter trip to Italy in November. I had always traveled independently and was not sure if a structured tour would be to our liking, but it turned out to be a great success. We flew to Rome and were bused to the Hotel Monte Catini Terme. The hotel became our home for a week and we had daily guided tours of Tuscany. Florence, with its art treasures, was naturally our favorite; but the rolling lush countryside and other historic cities enhanced the itinerary. The only problem the whole time was trying to get presidential election results on the Italian stations. There seemed to be a vote count issue in Florida, but the situation could not be explained. We later found out that people in the States were equally confused. One night, out of news deprivation, I set the alarm for 4:00am to get an English-speaking channel. To my amazement, the selected program came up showing an Italian porn movie. With innocent shock, I awoke Julia and we witnessed things that required no knowledge of the language.

After that nocturnal encounter, we needed a day free from the guides. We rented a car and drove to Pietrasanta and Carrara.

CHANGES PROFESSIONAL AND PERSONAL

This is where sculptors come from all over the world to study with the artigino or master carvers, and where Michelangelo obtained his marble for the David and other sculptures. We strolled agape like kids in Toyland and bought some of the fine crafted Milani carving tools and rasps.

The trip was an added highlight of the year and changed my view on chartered tours and we had a new U.S. President. Many of our fellow travelers were older acquaintances and getting to know them in a different setting made for even closer friendships. In fact we continued to have post-Tuscany parties to exchange pictures and experiences. The year began with a Y2K scare that never materialized and ended for us with the joyful feeling that it was the start of a new century.

12

Magical Travels

The next winter trip to Arizona had unexpected results. Once again we stayed at an Extended Stay Motel and despite having an efficiency suite, we began to question its practicality and the monthly expense. While on a drive to the Old West-styled town of Wickenburg to check on real estate, we stopped at the Sun City West tourist bureau. This retirement community was started in 1979, after the original Sun City was completed. I had always thought the over-55 concept was for unimaginative old people, but now that I was retired myself, my thinking had changed. We toured around with a broker and were much impressed by all that was offered.

We had had no intention of buying, but an opportunity came up that we could not refuse. The fates seemed to be showing the right path once again. This particular house was one of the newer, upgraded small models called *La Casita* and was fully landscaped. A Catholic priest was moving back to Wisconsin; as they say in the trade, he was a motivated seller. We ended up buying it fully stocked and furnished for a very reasonable price. It was an ideal move-in situation and the solution to spending another winter at a motel. During the period of financing and title searches, Father invited us to his St. Patrick's Day party. It was a traditional, festive affair that gave us the opportunity to meet our new neighbors and establish confidence in our hasty purchase. We closed on the property just before heading back east and would not see it again until the following January.

The summer was filled with the usual gardening, art activities, and visits with friends. Several of my classmates from Massachusetts Maritime were planning to take a weeklong cruise to Bermuda. I had spent enough time at sea and didn't think this trip would be worthwhile, but I let myself be cajoled. Once more I was proved completely wrong. We all had a wonderful time. The Norwegian cruise ship was our adult playground and it gave us a chance to really socialize. Bermuda had become more congested than when I had seen it earlier; the pace was quicker, but the beauty still captivating. During the last night of the trip we all gathered with the captain in one of the lounges and jokingly told him we had enough qualified merchant mariners to take over the ship. This innocent comment would have put us in serious trouble if it had been stated a week later, for the next day 9\11 occurred.

After the holidays, my daughter, Kimberly and her family moved to Florida. They agreed to take our dog Daisy, for she had worn out her welcome with all the others who had cared for her during previous trips. We would return via Florida in the spring to pick Daisy up. We all departed on the same day; they to a new home in the South and we to a new home in the West.

Our arrival was joyous as we opened the door and had the same rush of positive feelings as when we first saw the house.

Everything was in order and we found extra supplies and items that Father had generously left behind. Each day was like a rewarding treasure hunt.

The winter was spent getting used to our new abode. After a while I decided to expose Julia to another area of the country. Most of her travel during the navy days, had been in Europe and Japan, so she was eager to see the USA. We drove to San Diego past the sand dunes of Yuma and across the bountiful Imperial Valley. Arrival in San Diego was met with a little nostalgia for both of us, because of the ocean and strong naval presence. A visit to the zoo and a drive along the coast to La Jolla and the Scripps Institution of Oceanography brought back memories to me of an earlier visit. We returned home via Palm Springs. It proved to be another enjoyable exploratory adventure.

Our first winter in the new *casita* went by too quickly and soon it was time to head back to our other home. We closed up the Arizona house and arranged for a friend to keep an eye on things during our absence. We drove back as planned along the Gulf Coast into Florida and back up the East Coast, visiting friends in Florida as well as my daughter. After a brief but pleasant Florida stop, we rounded up a happy but confused dog and headed north.

It was a typical active summer, but the usual fall activities were cut short by an early cross-country departure for Sun City West. We had joined the New England Club, and one of its main social events was a full catered Thanksgiving dinner in the Desert Mountains. We, including our well-seasoned traveling dog, arrived in time for this eagerly awaited event and were not disappointed.

After enjoying our first Arizona Christmas, we excitedly prepared for January guests. My brother and his wife arrived from

Australia, as did my wife's daughter and friend. It was fun showing them around and wonderful to have everybody together. John found that Arizona reminded him of Australia.

Donald "Ben" Hogan, an academy classmate who was living near the Mexican border, had spent over thirty years with the Smithsonian Institution's telescope program. He arranged a special guided tour of the observatory on Mount Hopkins. Because it involved driving up a narrow winding road to over 8000 feet, only my brother and I went along. We went into areas and experienced things that no regular tour could provide.

That winter Julia and I purchased a car through an estate sale. Our plan was to fly back in October and use the car as our Arizona vehicle. After an eight month stay we packed up and departed for another long drive to the East Coast. A tape reading of the book *Memoirs of a Geisha* helped pass the time. A stopover for a few days with Larry and Millie Marsden in North Carolina and a route change to the Cape May Ferry also added an enjoyable diversion.

After an active summer, before we knew it, it was time to return to Arizona. The day of departure can only be described as last minute hectic. Previous trips were made easy in that the car acted as our mobile suitcase. Things were just thrown in willy nilly; the only concern was to leave space for Daisy Dog. This time we were flying. Four boxes packed with "nonessentials" had been shipped in advance, in order for us to meet the various luggage restrictions. And of course we had to have a travel kennel for the dog. I have shipped thousands of pounds of lobsters all over the world, but a 50-pound dog was a first. We spent weeks trying to get Daisy prepared. Initially she had a primordial fear of the carrier. Someone suggested placing a dish of peanut butter at the rear with other enticements. Then Daisy would have to spend time licking and licking the sticky concoction, and in the process she would become accustomed to her surroundings. To my surprise, the strategy seemed to work. The kennel was festooned with "This Side Up. Live Animal, My Name Is Daisy. Destination..." It reminded me of those old stickered suitcases you'd see in a B movie. The confusion of departure was also compounded by the fact that we were renting out the Magnolia house and had to do last minute-cleaning. Despite months of preparation, things were left to the last minute... chaos reigned.

Our car had been placed on jack stands in the garage and was being used as a storage locker. Julia's fine china items and my trusty old computer were stowed for the winter. We had arranged for a friend to transport us to Logan Airport. The bags were loaded. Daisy was sedated and placed in her travel kennel. We arrived on time and a redcap assisted us at the curb. We said our goodbyes as the large bags were checked through to Detroit and on to Phoenix. Our carry-ons and the dog kennel were wheeled into the lobby. Daisy had to be inspected and ticketed at the counter. She was listed as Priority Pet and her one-way fare was more than one of our round trips. Oh, the joy of pet ownership. The flight to Detroit went smoothly and a pretzel snack filled our gastronomic needs. My only concern was the Red Sox vs. Yankees score. However the one-hour changeover became two, because our connecting plane had a malfunction. We were paged and informed that Daisy was fine, but because of the heat and time delay she needed to be transferred to a bigger kennel at no charge. Priority Pet came to the rescue. The connecting plane could not be repaired so a replacement had to be found. We finally had to hike what seemed to be a hundred football fields with our awkward carry-on luggage. If I had only thought to use the overhead people-transit train, but "what do I know"?

We arrived in Phoenix only a few hours late to a temperature of 85 degrees and were met by a neighbor at the baggage claim area. (Any temperature over this amount would have resulted in pet embargo, so we lucked out.) Our bags and personal dog kennel miraculously appeared on the carousel, and even more amazing was the arrival of Daisy in the Priority Pet kennel.

The ride to our home in Sun City West was quite a cultural shock. Earlier in the day we had been scrambling with last-minute packing while the wind and waves performed as the result of an offshore storm. Now the desert night and shadowed mountain vista performed on a different stage. This rapid adjustment was so unlike our previous trips when we spent five days on the road gradually getting the feel of changing America.

As the temperature climbed, we experienced eight record-breaking days of more than 100 degrees. My new computer arrived with a malfunctioning keyboard, and three of our shipped boxes were damaged. But we soon settled into our Southwest lifestyle, and once again the New England Club had its Thanksgiving dinner in the mountains.

13

Interstate 40

Interstate 40 starts in Barstow, California and ends on the east coast of North Carolina. We left Sun City West on June 4th of 2004 and picked up route 40 in Holbrook, Arizona. The temperature was climbing to 110 degrees, so connecting through cool pine country seemed the best way to start Day One of our trip back to Massachusetts. It was a special relief for our dog Daisy. When we had traveled this area a month before, prominent signs everywhere warned: "No Camp Fires - High Fire Risk". The news on this day reported all roads in this area closed because of dangerous forest fires. Even the observatory on Mount Graham was threatened. This is one of the largest stands of ponderosa pines in the world. I guess someone got careless or just didn't care.

Holbrook is on the Navaho Indian reservation and is the gateway to the dinosaur and Petrified Forest area. It is hard to imagine that this open rangeland long ago was extremely active and under the sea. Once on the interstate, with a speed limit of 75 mph, the 3000-mile trip back east really began. We spent first night in Grants, New Mexico. This Indian uranium-mining town has been turned into a motel mecca. We had stopped here before, so we knew the motels that accepted dogs. (Advanced dog-motel planning on our trips had become a traveling preoccupation.) The weather was in the seventies, but we were still cold after leaving the hot desert climate. The nearby 4B's Restaurant had just made a pot of their famous tomato soup and it was a warm welcome. The recipe can be found on the Internet, just Google "4B's Tomato Soup Recipe" and you will find some surprising ingredients.

Day Two began with a call from one of our neighbors who had moved to Albuquerque and we made plans to meet for breakfast on our way through. It was nice to be able to catch up with Eliza Sparks and her new life in New Mexico. After breakfast we continued up to the high plain area of Tucumcari, then down to the "Don't Mess with Texas" state line and on to Amarillo for the night. We had scheduled an early check-in so that we could root for the Kentucky Derby winner, Smarty Jones. The Triple Crown awaited him; however, he lost to the long shot Birdsong. Ronald Reagan also lost his battle with Alzheimer's that night.

Day Three took us across the Panhandle. In Groom, Texas we stopped to view the largest bronze cross in the western hemisphere. It is surrounded by detailed life size Stations of the Cross - one man's gift for everyone to view. The story goes that a despondent trucker was contemplating suicide until he came upon this highway sighting.

The weather was staying favorable despite threats of violent thunderstorms and tornadoes. Driving through Oklahoma we watched for the gooney-bird oil rigs pumping away. They are indeed strange and amusing sights. Arkansas was next, with an early dinner stop at Colson's Steak House in Russellville, just outside

Little Rock. I liked this place because along with the good steaks they served as an appetizer roasted peanuts in a big tin bucket. You are expected to discard your shells on the floor to add to the rustic ambience; for some reason I found this psychologically relieving. We spent the night in Lonoke, Arkansas, only 100 miles from Memphis.

On Day Four we crossed the mighty Mississippi and continued on through Tennessee, listening to a tape of the O.J. Simpson civil trial. The verdict was GUILTY. A few minor showers appeared in Nashville and Knoxville, and the day ended in Sevierville. Tomorrow was to be our crossing over the Great Smoky Mountains into Asheville, North Carolina.

Day Five saw us winding up the mountain road and through the tunnels. The road is a most spectacular Interstate 40 engineering accomplishment, rivaled only by the scenery. We had planned on visiting Jack Connors, another friend who had moved from our Arizona neighborhood. We had hoped to be the first guests at his new mountain house, but a little mix-up in plans prevented our meeting. Instead, we spent the time touring the Biltmore Estate. What an incredible break in our cross-country trek! The 8000 acres designed by Frederick Law Olmsted of Central Park fame, comprise formal gardens, natural and exotic plantings, and vineyards surrounding the largest private residence in the country. George Vanderbilt, grandson of shipping tycoon Cornelius, was more interested in beauty and the arts than in commerce. In 1895 his dreams of a modest mountain retreat ended with thousands of workmen building a four acre home covering 175,000 square feet with 250 rooms, including 31 guest rooms and 65 fireplaces. A 20,000-volume library and art treasures from around the world added elegance to this magnificent estate. The stable's large box stalls had been turned into unique individual dining rooms. We had a pleasant lunch there and ended the day tasting wine at the private winery. The local Best Western Motel, rather a step down from the day's splendor, accepted dogs. We humbly spent the night watching TV and munching on delivered pizza.

Day Six began with a call to *USS Doyen* friend, Larry Marsden in High Point, North Carolina. We had previously planned on spending an overnight with him and Millie on our way through the Tarheel state. Everything worked out well and we relished our lunch at a local seafood restaurant. Julia and I, having been in seafood-deprived Arizona all winter, had been looking forward to some tasty scallops and oysters. I must say, seeing the Marsdens and enjoying the seafood was a dual treat. After lunch Larry showed us around the changing area. The ubiquitous Wal-Marts and Costcos were now replacing most of the once thriving mills.

Daisy and the Marsden's dog, Muffy, enjoyed a reunion as well. Daisy was even allowed to stay in the house overnight. Before the cocktail hour, we all took naps that helped prepare us for the newly discovered Grey Goose vodka. We enjoyed steaks on the patio accompanied by Australian Black Swan red wine. Fireflies flitted about on the riverbank, signaling the end of a wonderful day.

Day Seven opened with breakfast of ham and eggs. Larry read aloud my recent article on Earl Brizard for the MMA Bulletin. His editorial approval added to my satisfaction in writing this piece. Before our departure we were introduced to their new entertainment center. Sound and picture were very effective, especially in a preview of the dramatic movie, *Master and Commander*. We said our goodbyes, accompanied by warm, heartfelt hugs.

INTERSTATE 40

Back onto I-40 we headed east to my old Duke University stomping grounds. It was hard to imagine that fifty years had gone by. On impulse, we tried to locate an old Essex, Massachusetts, friend who was in a Wake Forest nursing home. Her sister lived in the town, but I had no number or address. When we had no luck finding Barbara, we went off on country roads to connect with Interstate 95 north in Rocky Mount and up to Suffolk, Virginia. We ruled out taking I-95 through Washington because of the Reagan funeral service next day, and instead headed east to Norfolk and the Chesapeake Bay Bridge Tunnel. When passing the Peanut Patch outlet, I recalled my peanut passion, and we made a stop. After missing the Bridge Tunnel turnoff we ended up in the Virginia Beach boardwalk area. It was nice to finally see the Atlantic Ocean, but I preferred a better viewing. This we got when we crossed over and under Hampden Roads and entered the Eastern Shore. Dinner and more good seafood awaited us. We had trouble finding a motel that accepted dogs, and ended up driving longer and later than we had intended. Finally near Pocomoke, Maryland, we settled for the night and watched some of the Reagan preparations.

Day Eight started off gray and drizzly. Our plan to go up the Garden State Parkway via the Cape May ferry changed with the bad weather. I had always wanted to go out to Chincoteague Island, but time had never allowed this side trip. We were in no hurry now, so we went across the causeway to the quaint intercoastal town. I was surprised to find a major NASA tracking and launch site along the way. After breakfast we drove to where the "Horses of Chincoteague" swim to the mainland. But the gate said, "No Dogs," so we had to do a turnaround. We were in a pristine environmentally protected area, so the restriction was understandable. I could also see, by looking at the surrounding marshes, why the area is famous for its oyster production. We headed back to the mainland and set a course for Annapolis.

My dream as a young man had been to go to the U.S. Naval Academy. Things worked out much better, for I experienced Duke University and later the Massachusetts Maritime Academy. Still, I did want at least to see Annapolis. Julia had been there many times, but after reading *Dark Side*, a murder mystery set at the academy, my own curiosity was heightened. The drive around the academy satisfied my life's desire and my pride in graduating from MMA even greater. The day was special for me, and our proximity to the Reagan - Washington funeral was equally important. Although we decided not to attempt going into the capitol, we were moved to try being nearby and following the service on the radio.

We spent the late afternoon trying to find a house in Crofton, Maryland where Julia had once lived. Fortunately a man in a convenience store remembered the original 40 year old development and led us to the exact street. The surrounding trees had matured and things looked different, but we did find Julia's house. Some of her plants were now fully grown. We were tempted to knock on the door and meet the current owners, but motored on. Another lifetime put in the memory bank.

Instead of going through the old Baltimore tunnel, we went around on I-695 and over the Key Bridge, named after Francis Scott Key of "Star Spangled Banner" fame. Fort McHenry and the shipyards of Baltimore were seen in the distance. My experiences in these shipyards returned, even flashback memories of seeing the infamous Blaze Starr.

We located a satisfactory motel in Edgewater and watched the return of President Reagan to Simi Valley for his final rest. The service was very moving with the TV capturing the sun as it sank dramatically in the west and closed out his life. Our day ended as well, but we hope for many, many more to follow.

Day Nine was bringing us into the home stretch. The continental breakfast, one of our better ones, helped ready us for the Delaware Memorial Bridge and the boring New Jersey Turnpike. The plan of the day was to find Livingston, New Jersey, and Erle Brizard's MMA classmate, Mario Guidette. I had followed up Erle's article with an interview with Mario, due to be published in the September *Bulletin*. I was hoping to meet Mario in person, but fate intervened. We found Livingston, but Mario had an unlisted number and unfortunately I had not packed the number or his street address. As you can see, some of my best-laid plans were not fully organized. The final leg brought us to Hartford for the night.

Day Ten arrived with still a little time before our visit the next day with Julia's daughter. So a trip to the Mohegan Sun Casino added a little diversion to our cross-country adventure. We passed many reservation casinos on the way, but nothing compared to the elaborate Sun. The architecture and use of space for art and eye appeal was amazing. One does not have to be a gambler to appreciate this creation. Jasper White's offered more seafood temptation. We had oysters on the half shell and chowder; a departing hit on the slots helped pay the bill. The ride up the old Blackstone Valley to the Mass. Turnpike brought back an era of mill activity long gone. We stopped for the night near Julia's daughter - a morning visit was planned. We contacted our tenants in Magnolia, who were leasing until June 15th, and made arrangements for our arrival.

Waking early on Day Eleven, I went off to the local Jiffy Lube. The car was performing well, but needed grease and oil and tire change. When the car was ready, we headed to Lisa's in Hopkinton. Julia's first meeting with her only grandchild showed promise of many more happy times. After lunch and a stroll, we departed for our final destination, Cape Ann, only to find dog restrictions and ridiculous $140 plus room rates. Although our tenants were leaving in the morning we were trapped like tourists. Finally, in that it was an off night, one motel operator altered the rules and offered us reasonably priced accommodations.

Day Twelve was finally our homecoming. We went over to the house to say goodbye to our tenants. As it turned out, they liked the house so much that they asked if they could come back from October until June next year. What a relief, the house was clean and well cared for, and there would be no need to screen new tenants. Daisy remembered old smells and places, but we spent the next week trying to find items we had packed away. Finally all settled in and the summer went by quickly. An old saying comes to mind, "Fourth of July, an ear of corn and summers gone." It makes one realize that time is fleeting and that one needs to capture and prize every minute. Our return trip to Arizona in October will be by air and only hours, not days. Will we travel across this beautiful country again next June? Probably. After all, Larry, Millie and Muffy expect us.

14

Driving Miss Daisy Dog

The October 2006 departure date for our drive back to Arizona was fast approaching and Daisy Dog was showing signs of old age. Arthritis had settled in the old joints, and walking was becoming a major chore. Julia and I had agreed that we would not let her painfully suffer and would act accordingly when the time was obvious. A visit to the vet relieved our concerns, because she received a clean bill of health and given the OK to make the five to six day trip. In fact, there seemed to be a dramatic uplift in her spirits and agility as we started packing. Maybe she was aware of the soothing warm dry air ahead and NO MORE STAIRS to navigate.

Surprisingly we got off on time at 9:00am on the 10th and headed to our first stop in Livingston, N.J. We had kept in touch with Mario Guidette, Massachusetts Maritime Academy's oldest living graduate, ever since I wrote an article on his merchant marine and WWII careers. A 1928 graduate of the old training-school ship *Nantucket* at 98 years young he still maintained his own home. We had missed seeing him on previous trips, now we were finally here. It was an emotional lunch visit and very mean-ingful, but brief because we had "miles to go before we sleep" and I was anxious to head west out of the congestion. Our first stop was Fogelsville, Pennsylvania on the outskirts of Allentown in the historic Lehigh Valley. The Comfort Inn lived up to its name as we settled in to complete the first travel day. Even Daisy Dog slept through the night with only one outdoor visit.

Checkout went well, except that Daisy probably should have had more nocturnal walks. She left a very large liquid impression on the motel walkway as soon as we left the lobby. Julia thought it resembled a giraffe; I saw the definite influence of abstract artists de Kooning and Rothko.

It seemed that art would be with us all day as we traveled over the Susquehanna River at Harrisburg and followed the Pennsyl-vania Turnpike through the Allegheny Mountain region. The fall foliage created a riot of color on nature's palette and we drove all day in constant pleasure. Our new 140-channel satellite radio also provided pleasure because we no longer had only sporadic recep-tion. We lost touch with Fox News or beautiful music only when passing through the amazingly engineered mountain tunnels. The turnpike was the grandfather of interstate travel and the seven tunnels bored through the mountains in the late 1930s are still a wonder today.

My geography got a little confused at this point. I thought we should have entered Ohio before West Virginia. However, no one had reshuffled the states. Our routing had simply taken us through the narrow northern section of West Virginia. We quickly entered Wheeling and then crossed the Ohio River. The Buckeye State line soon appeared, reassuring me that my geog-raphy was not too far off. After a look at the map we quickly decided to go straight through Columbus on I-70 instead of the following beltway. The city is rich in art, and for golf fans Ohio State University houses the Jack Nicklaus Museum and his six Masters trophies. There is also a full-scale replica of the *Santa Maria*, Christopher Columbus' flag ship. Coincidentally, we were passing through on Columbus Day, but I must admit I have low regard for Chris because of the atrocities he committed in the New Land. Another example of how history can be distorted.

But I digress. Onward west through Dayton, birthplace of the Wright brothers, and we hoped to reach the Indiana state line. Unfortunately the sky turned an ominous swirling black and heavy rain destroyed the visibility. It looked as if we were driving (sailing) off the end of the world. Luckily the next exit ramp brought us to the safety of the Ramada Inn. Its big neon sign was like a beacon. After drying Daisy we feasted on snacks from the car and settled in for the night.

We heard on the news that we had witnessed a cluster of tornadoes. Damage had occurred around the Dayton area and we were not even in "Tornado Alley" yet! The available movie that night, a great diversion from the recent scare, was based on the life of golf legend Bobby Jones. The characters of golfing professional Walter Hagen and sports writer, Grantland Rice were played very well, and the authentic wooden clubs and scenes of Saint Andrews added to the drama. I was not aware that despite peer pressure Jones had never turned pro, and had won all his victories as an amateur. He replied to the angry professionals by saying that the definition of amateur is to "play to enjoy the game and not for monetary gain". All sports could use more of his integrity. After retiring from competition, he took a bit of rough

Georgia land and created the Augusta National Golf Club, the official site of the Masters.

The following morning I let Julia and Daisy sleep a little longer and wandered down to the hot complimentary breakfast room. I knew that "hot" meant a waffle machine would be available and I wanted to do my culinary thing. The batter was pre-measured and the instructions seemed pretty simple (if you read them). I poured batter onto the grill and turned the unit full on, thinking to heat the waffle on both sides. Upon later reading, the instruction was a slight turn to start the heating process. Most of my batter flowed out of the overturned grill into a waiting tray. My waffles looked like golden brown crepes on the bottom with a gooey batter on top. I was too embarrassed to repeat the process, so I loaded up on syrup to disguise my flipping failure.

We departed after sharing a safe, conventional continental breakfast. Good driving weather ahead was predicted, and Indiana, despite construction warnings, presented no problems. It was like getting the Indy racing checker flag. We went through Indianapolis, again avoiding the beltway, and followed up on the morning *USA* newspaper report of a major local event. The headline read, *PATH TO SAINTHOOD, Indiana nun's amazing story. There are nuns and then there are nuns. And then there's Blessed Mother Theodore-Guerin. She brought Catholic education to Indiana, endured an overbearing bishop, and is believed for at least two "miracles" after her death... Pope Benedict XVI will canonize Mother Theodore, along with three others, Sunday in Saint Peter's Square in Rome, making her America's eighth Catholic saint... Born in France in 1798, she left for America... Traveling by steamboat, canal and eventually stagecoach, she arrived at Indiana's wooded and uninhabited western frontier with no money or English skills. Undeterred she started several schools and founded the congregation*

Sisters of Providence and a girls' academy. The school, a few miles west of Terra Haute, has since become Saint Mary-of-the-Woods College, the oldest Catholic liberal arts college for women.

All of Julia's grade school and high school teaching nuns graduated from this college, so it was of special interest.

We entered St. Louis, Missouri by crossing over the mighty Mississippi. The Eero Saarinen Gateway Arch to the West loomed 630 feet into the skyline. Any thought of confining ourselves in a plastic cocoon for a ride to the top to view the surroundings was quickly dispelled by Julia's expression. Rivers were becoming a fixation. We had crossed the Hudson, Delaware, Allegheny, Susquehanna, Ohio, Wabash, Mississippi and the Missouri and still more waited ahead. Although their north-south flows were entirely opposed to our longitudinal pursuit, I had the urge to some day just follow these rivers and get a different perspective on America.

This same feeling was experienced by one of my favorite writers, William Least Heat-Moon when he traveled the country. He, in fact, did explore the rivers and wrote the book *River Horse: A Voyage into America*. Speaking of Least Heat, it was his book *PrairyErth*, a deep study of Chase County, Kansas that had inspired my plotted route to Arizona. The book had been described as our modern-day *Walden* and *the Moby Dick* of American history. I just had to travel through Kansas to personally experience this new-found divination. But first Missouri lay ahead. Travel went well and as we passed by Columbia, home of the university. I recalled that this is the area where Least Heat lives and teaches English Literature. (It was pointed out to me years ago when I showed an interest in writing, that Missouri and Iowa had the best creative writing programs.) The day ended in Independence, home of one of our favorite presidents, Harry S Truman.

Waking up in Harry and Bess's hometown was an unexpected pleasure. We visited the presidential library and got good pictures of a large bronze teddy bear sitting with legs akimbo and reading an old newspaper. The headline: DEWEY DEFEATS TRUMAN. We also shot pictures of the summer White House and Kansas City Royals sports complex before crossing the Missouri River from Kansas City, Missouri, into Kansas City, Kansas. The divided city was another of those confusing geographical enigmas.

We were finally in Kansas. Dorothy's statement to Toto from *The Wizard of Oz* came to mind: "There's no place like home." Previous travels through the state had been uneventful and unnoticed because we were just trying to get across the vast space to get to the Denver area. This time, we had a purpose in mind and headed for Chase County. At Topeka we got off the interstate and headed southwest through corn, cotton and wheat fields to Cottonwood Falls and the Flint Hills.

This area is geographically almost the center of the nation and the last grand expanse of tall grass prairie in America. Whereas it once constituted only 4 percent of the American long grass prairie, now it is virtually all that is left. The grasses can grow to ten feet - so high the Indians once had to stand on their horses to see ahead. The hills are made of limestone and shale and never rise more than three hundred feet, but their length and breadth spreads eighty miles wide through most of the two-hundred-mile longitude of Kansas from Nebraska to Oklahoma. At one time this area was part of the Permian Sea. If humans had lived here fifty million years ago, they could have paddled from Pittsburgh to Denver

The Tallgrass Prairie National Preserve is the only part of the national park system dedicated to this rich and cultural history.

DRIVING MISS DAISY DOG

While only 11,000 acres remain of what once covered 400,000 square miles of central North America, here we could view the rolling hills and wide-open vistas and imagine the activities of the Kansa and Osage Indian hunting parties. A cycle of climate, fire, and animal grazing (once buffalo, now cattle) has sustained this ecosystem. I completely agree with the preserve's statement that "much of the grassland flora and fauna is too subtle to be seen from a passing car, but careful scrutiny reveals the special beauty, wonder and complexity of the prairie".

My brother John, a professional photographer from Australia, introduced me to William Least Heat-Moon and this magical area. John photographed here two years previously, but the negatives and pictures were destroyed in shipment back to Australia. As if he had a calling, he was compelled to return and shoot again and it turned out the second pictures showed more intense feeling and knowledge. I had wanted to find out for myself what drove John and Least Heat to what I thought as a barren, stark land. As Julia and I gazed about and truly reflected on the landscape, we as artists understood and could appreciate the greater meaning. Julia and I had a similar experience on the Hopi reservation in Arizona. At that time, the inexplicable pull was so strong that we felt the urge to blissfully renew our marriage vows in Walpi, one of oldest mesas.

John had made several friends in Cottonwood Falls and we made a point of calling on them. The owner of the Grand Central Hotel, Susan Barnes, greeted us and proudly told us that her son, Zak, was having a major art opening in Kansas City. Zak's paintings expressed the Flint Hills in a manner that only someone in tune with his surroundings could truly capture. We of course took pictures of the area. One in particular of Daisy and me posing in front of the county court house was significant because she gracefully timed a "dump" at the moment of exposure. Our other pictures could never equal my brother's professionalism, but "point and shoot" sometimes brought surprising results. We had achieved our travel objective. Looking back, I realize that we could never fully grasp the tall grass prairie and Flint Hills in only one afternoon of observation, Still, to quote Henry David Thoreau, "New earths, new themes expect us".

The night stop in Wichita brought us back to reality. This is the fifty-first largest city in America and is known as the Air Capital because of the numerous aircraft manufacturing facilities. Driving around trying to find the pet-accommodating Best Western was a little confusing, but it proved to be a good motel. We had looked forward to having the dining room conveniently on the premises, but were disappointed when the management decided to make Friday nights strictly a full buffet. We opted for snacks in the room and watched the Detroit Tigers beat the Oakland A's. Our inside room faced the pool area and a huge recreation room that housed Ping Pong and pool tables, as well as a shuffleboard, carousel, putting green, and video arcade. Despite the proximity of these activities we all had a good night's sleep.

After a disappointing breakfast buffet (included in the room fare), we were on our way. We traveled by an area that would soon be home to hundreds of thousands of migrating sand hill cranes. I read in the *Wichita News* that the National Kansas Wetlands Wildlife Scenic Byway, a 76-mile drive, was soon to be dedicated. *National Geographic* was producing a new travel directory listing 290 of the best drives in the nation and it would include the Kansas drive. The magic continued! Since I am touting the sunflower state, let me mention a few of the Kansans who helped changed the world: Dwight D. Eisenhower, Bob Dole, and Amelia Earhart. With places like the infamous Last Chance Saloon, I should also include Carrie Nation and her crusade against "demon rum".

The next segment of our Kansas experience was totally unexpected. I never would have believed that there could be a meaningful sequel to the prairie exposure, but strange things happen when you travel. A look at the route from Wichita to the Oklahoma and Texas panhandle showed a place called Liberal, home of the film site of *The Wizard of Oz*. We planned only a quick stop, expecting a touristy setup, but were completely surprised and impressed. The city's name in itself was odd and certainly not in our political vocabulary. Its origin lay in 1872 when western Kansas consisted of mile after mile of waving prairie grasslands and one large flowing river. Outside of the Cimarron River, water was very scarce and settlers traveling west on the Santa Fe Trail were usually charged a fee. Mr. S.S.Rogers, one of the first homesteaders, always gave his water free to passing travelers. Quite often he would hear the reply, "that's mighty liberal of you" from the grateful recipients. In 1885 Mr. Rogers opened a general store and the government established an official post office. It seemed only natural to call the new town "Liberal".

After a lunch of finally tasty barbecue ribs, we visited the Wizard of Oz Museum and Dorothy's home movie site. We were especially fortunate to be following the yellow brick road today because once a year the Museum holds a costume competition for all the characters. The Dorothy award is the most coveted, but young and old were in the spirit and we were surrounded by wicked witches, Auntie Ems, tin men, straw men, and fairy queens. Even the original Munchkins were there for photo signing. Julia was grabbed and hugged by the cowardly lion. He obviously got up some courage after seeing such startling beauty. Daisy was also in for a treat because she met many Toto lookalikes. The winner of the Dorothy contest was quite alarmed when Daisy tried to climb into Toto's basket. Despite Daisy's squirming attempts, the wicker would not yield to accommodate a long-eared black basset with a Labrador head. One of the Auntie Ems came along with a whiskbroom to shoo her away. It was a comical unexpected break in the trip for all of us. I am sure Daisy never imagined she would be following the yellow brick road and go "over the rainbow" to the Emerald City. I know that we had not planned such a fantasy. As I have said many times, "Never take a trip, let the trip take you".

The drive out of Liberal brought us through small farming and cattle towns. Many had tall corn mazes set up in the fields for children to playfully figure how to get in and out. I couldn't resist calling this "Amazing Fun", but was upstaged down the road by a farmer who called his creation, "Amazing Grace". As we went through the panhandle, foul-smelling feed lots became prominent. I suppose that is the smell of money to some people, but it is certainly offensive to passing travelers. The anti-litter road sign, "Don't Mess with Texas", went unnoticed by Daisy. As soon as we crossed the state line she had the urge to fertilize the sacred ground. Her nature's call might have been motivated by the aromatic feedlots. As we approached our destination for the night (Tucumcari, New Mexico), a violent wind and rain storm came up. We checked in without any problems and retired, realizing we were within a day's ride of home. The Tigers won the American League Pennant and Daisy slept peacefully throughout the night, probably dreaming of Toto or chewing on Dorothy's red slippers.

DRIVING MISS DAISY DOG

After breakfast at K-Bob's we were back on Interstate 40. Most of the trip was without hazard, but outside Albuquerque I found myself squeezed by two unrelenting semis in an unexpected construction lane change. It was a close call and so near to our final destination. We passed through Albuquerque looking skyward for colorful hot air balloons. A festival had been scheduled, but apparently there was a weather cancellation. We continued up to the Navaho town of Gallup and again faced a blinding rainstorm. After a truck-stop lunch that defied imagination, we continued on I-40 to Flagstaff.

It was here that we turned south on I-17 for Phoenix. The elevation dropped from 7000 feet to around 1000 as we approached Sun City West. Once again, after 3000 miles of travel, we were safely back in the "compound". We found everything in great condition, thanks to friend and neighbor Vern Irby. His wife, Fran, had thoughtfully put orange juice and homemade apricot bread in the refrigerator. Our goldfish had not multiplied like last year and they greeted us with gulping mouths, as only fish can do. Daisy was ecstatic to find no stairs to encounter and immediately looked for rabbits to chase and coyotes to challenge. Life at Paradise Found was beginning a new season.

15

Tale of the Splintered Paddle

Many cross-country trips and side adventures followed over the years, but before attempting a conclusion, I would like to keep the magic in place and describe a more recent trip.

A return visit to the Big Island of Hawaii had always been on my wish list, but it wasn't until 2006 that I was able to have another adventure there - one that involved me with the legendary warrior-king, Kamehameha.

My wife, Julia and I made our reservations from Sun City West in January, and I also notified Paul Driscoll, an old Maritime Academy friend who had retired in Waikoloa Village on the Big Island after twenty years with the Massachusetts State Police. His nick name, "Baddog" came from his expertise in training and tracking with bloodhounds. He was excited about our visit and promised a grand tour of his north side of the island.

The months went by rapidly and the April 8th departure day finally arrived. Despite the strong trade winds we arrived in Kona on schedule and had to debark onto the tarmac from the portable steep steps. It was just like in the old movies. Remember the scenes from Casablanca? The Kona airport, with its open air lobby, was as I remembered it thirty-three years before. At this point, I think the magic pull of the island was setting in again. I felt a familiar sense of belonging. In our compact rental Chevrolet Cobra we took a few side trips along the Kona coast on our way to the Hotel Manago. It was disappointing to see the rise of box stores like Home Depot and Wal-Mart. They tried to hide them from the highway behind foliage, but they were there. One particular diversion was a lush four mile road leading 2500 feet down to Kealakekau Bay, "Path of the Gods". Julia exclaimed that it was like really being in the jungle. The Bay is a marine sanctuary and the area where British discoverer, Captain Cook was slain by the natives. When he first arrived he was mistaken as a God; but when his ship had to return because of bad weather, the natives recognized his mortality and a fatal uprising occurred. A statue marks the spot but it is not accessible by rental car. Farther along we visited one of the many Kona coffee factory outlets. Coffee was introduced to the islands by the missionaries in the 1800s and thrived on the Kona hillsides. The smell of roasted coffee permeated the air and contrasted nicely with other tropical fragrances.

We arrived at the quaint native family hotel around five o'clock. I had stayed here many years ago and found nothing had changed except the eighty-five year old owner, Harold Manago, had turned over the operation to his son. The koi pond still supported colorful fish that were probably swimming about when I last visited. We crossed over a covered bridge from the lobby to our room. It had a lanai overlooking a lush hillside that ran down to the Pacific Ocean. Terraced gardens, flowering jacaranda, and various fruit trees provided a palette that would have pleased the

TALE OF THE SPLINTERED PADDLE

Masters. Barking dogs and crowing roosters from the village below filled the air and added to the island mystique.

The next morning, breakfast was a pleasant surprise. Along with the fresh tropical fruit we were served Portuguese sausage with the local eggs. I have had linguica and chorizo back in Gloucester and New Bedford, but nothing as big and tasty as this island version.

Our next adventure was driving down the narrow winding Napoopo'o road to the City of Refuge. This sacred area was where law breakers were purified and ancient Hawaiians sought political asylum. The nearby beach was where the traditional outrigger canoe races were held. Our friend, Paul, participated in the race and the kama'aina, old time Hawaiians, claimed he could compete and row with the best of them. In fact, as a result of his in-depth knowledge derived from the Maritime Academy and personal experimentation he is writing a book on paddle displacement. Excerpts from the book have created a major controversy among the paddling purists.

The road back up to the main highway was like driving through a tunneled tropical wonderland. As we approached South Point, the terrain changed to the Ka'u district with its bleak terrain and old lava flows. We decided not to drive down just to say we had been there, but I should note that it is the southernmost tip of the United States and located 19 degrees north of the equator. To put it in perspective, this is on latitude that runs 500 miles south of Miami.

After passing the Black Sand Beach, we stopped at the Volcano Visitor Center. This facility is operated by the National Park Service and provides a wealth of information on volcanic activity. We had lunch in the Volcano House Hotel over looking Kilauea Crater and stayed to view several of the educational presentations.

Our drive to the second largest Hawaiian city was a culture shock after the auto dealerships and shopping malls. The downtown was old and interesting and set back from the large bay. A tsunami in 1946 had wiped out almost everything along the shore, so a scenic road provided nice open views. A large passenger ship, *The Pride of America* was in port. The first oceangoing ship to hoist the Stars and Stripes in nearly 50 years, she is sailing inter-island cruises. We learned from one of the passengers that another U.S. flagged ship is planned called, *The Pride of Hawaii.* The libraries of the old *SS America* and *SS United States* (Big U) are being installed on these ships to keep proud Merchant Marine continuity.

During the approach to the city we noticed that the Mauna Loa Macadamia Nut factory was open to visitors. The road in went through 2500 acres of nut trees. More than a century ago a sugar plantation manager introduced macadamia nuts to the island. Native to the Australian rain forest, the nuts thrived in Hawaii as well. It was a far-seeing Massachusetts man, Ernest Van Tassel who planted the first Hawaiian macadamia plantation on government land. The current modern factory and retail outlet carried every conceivable variation of the nut. It was learned that Hershey had bought out the factory which explained the presence of many chocolate creations as well.

Before checking into the hotel we visited Hilo Hattie's, the largest manufacturer of "Aloha Wear". Julia, our hat fahionista had no luck finding an unusual hat; however, she did find a small grass skirt for granddaughter, Sofia. We foolishly posed, looking like Ma and Pa Kettle Go Hawaiian, for a photo in front of the largest muumuu in the world, but nothing could be funnier than the music and comedy of Clara Haili, better known as Hilo Hattie. Although mostly a novelty act, through the 1930s, 40s and 50s she recorded with many of the best musicians. Her songs include "South Sea Sadie", "Cockeyed Mayor of Kaunakaki", "Ukulele Lady" and my favorite, the ribald classic, "Princess Pupule Has Plenty Papayas... she loves to give them away." On a negative note, "Hilo Hattie" was apparently the code name for a covert military operation that helped lay the ground work for the Vietnam War.

Our new goal was to return to one of my favorite spots, the Waipi'o Valley. We crossed many one lane bridges with cascading waterfalls to the west and vast ocean views to the east. As we traveled further north, sugar cane fields lined both sides of the road. When we arrived at the overlook, nothing appeared to have changed since my last visit. However, there was an obvious changed in me. Before I had hiked down the steep 25 degree trail to the black sand beach, and then followed a river to the legendary waterfall. All I could do now was enjoy the view and walk partway down the trail. I was looking for a walking stick to help me get back up to the overlook {where Julia had wisely stayed} and to my amazement an abandoned sturdy stick was found. There were signs that the stick had been treated at one time. It was well worn at the bottom with a flared split at the top and had a strange aura. I thanked the gods for the find. Back at the overlook, I placed it in the trunk of the car wondering if I could bring it back on the plane.

The walking stick brought added excitement on the drive to Waimea where we would be meeting our friend Baddog Driscoll. I was anxious to get his opinion on my find. We were now traveling through cattle country home of the Parker Ranch. This vast spread started when a young Massachusetts boy, John Palmer Parker, jumped ship in 1847 and bought two acres from King

Kamehameha. With 175,000 tropical acres it is now the largest private ranch under single ownership in the country. Hawaiian cowboys called *paniolo* successfully work the ranch in a tradition out of the Wild West.

We checked into the Waimea Country Lodge and finally met the infamous Baddog in person. I thought of him as an old friend, but the relationship had really just grown over the past few years through e-mail and the Maritime Academy connection. The first time encounter was warm and meaningful; he looked just as the way we had envisioned a retired state cop that had gone native. His powerful muscular frame was enhanced by a long flowing grey pony tail and his animated gestures and talk was equal to his colorful prose.

In true Academy upper job style, I immediately put him to work to inspect the walking stick and clean it up. In true "youngie" fashion, he snapped to attention and began to carry out the order. Everything came to a rapid halt when he explained that the stick had been a racing paddle. The flared top was the hand grip and the rough splintered bottom had held the paddle. He said with excitement that he would take it home and clean it up and give the royal treatment it deserved. Imagine finding an old splintered paddle at the Valley of the Kings. My mystical involvement with the island continued when I learned that King Kamehameha had once proclaimed an edict called The Law of the Splintered Paddle. This law altered island history and is used today in international law. Briefly, it involves avoiding war time atrocities and protecting the innocent.

We spent the remainder of the day getting acquainted and going over old stories. The more Paul talked the more Julia and I thought that he must be a clone of Jonathan Winters. He treated us that evening to dinner at Merrimen's, one of the finer restaurants. He and Julia had prawns and a kind of Hawaiian quesadilla with goat cheese and mangos and I, missing good seafood, had a local fish called *ono*. We agreed to meet in the morning at the King's Shops in Waikoloa, and Paul returned home with the precious stick assignment.

After an old fashioned breakfast of oatmeal, raisins and brown sugar, our drive down to the coast brought us into the modern mall world. We met Paul in front of some fashionable stores near the Hilton Resort area. He was wildly waving my new walking stick which he had been cleaned and trimmed to fit a king. The hand grip was now fashioned from fancy rope work and there even was a flowing braided lanyard. Only a "deckie" could have created such a masterpiece for an upper job engineer. I think even Hawaiian Royalty would have felt honored.

We spent touring the North Kohala coast, an area that I had not previously explored. Here was King Kamehameha's birthplace and site of the original nine-foot bronze statue. I proudly went before the King and presented my "Stick of Knowledge". It might have been my imagination, but I think I saw his raised fingers move and in pleased recognition point down in my direction. With the stillness in the air, it was like being in a spiritual power center. I left the scene feeling as though I was carrying on ancient tradition.

Later we relaxed in a cabana at Rockefeller's Mauna Loa Beach Resort sipping cool mai tais before returning to the King's Shops. We said our goodbye hoping Paul would reciprocate and visit us in Arizona next year. In true island spirit, it seemed the walking stick had created a tight bond. All went well with security at the airport and I was allowed to carry the walking stick aboard the plane.

When checking in, one of Hawaiian security and agricultural inspectors noticed the stick and wanted to know if I had returned a favor to the Gods for removing something from the island. I acknowledged that I had, but little did he know of the spiritual exchange I had with King Kamehameha. The Law of the Splintered Paddle lives on with even greater meaning.

16

A Conclusion, but not a Final Conclusion

My hope is that my travels, tales, and observations will continue, but this book must have a conclusion. Vivian Wheeler and Marilynn Vita, my editors and grammatical gurus, are crying for mercy. I thought reflection on my recent 50th reunion at Massachusetts Maritime Academy would be a fitting tribute to events and friends of the past half century.

During my early writing experiences, personal computers, Word, Google and other such writing and research aids were unknown. I just relied on a journal, and my trusty Remington Rand typewriter traveled all over the world with me. The carry case was used as a miniature suitcase to store socks, underwear, toiletries and occasional nips. Keeping accurate records was almost impossible. Incomplete diaries, journal entries and notes on the back of ship daily menus were stored in old cigar boxes. Poems and ideas for sculpture projects were scribbled on whatever writing material was available. Unfortunately it usually was cocktail napkins that eventually became blurred and faded. Nevertheless, fragments became whole and this book captures most of the moments.

MANY LANDS MANY HEARTS

Many friends and acquaintances have come and gone with the tide and their marks have been etched in the sand. I will not mention names, just find your place in the pages and know that you have been loved and appreciated; however, I would be remiss in not mentioning my art teacher, Marie Ederne Jaeckel. It was her inspiration and guidance that gave me the encouragement to pursue sculpture and find my creative voice.

LaVergne, TN USA
28 February 2010
174501LV00001B/2/P